CONTENTS

ABOUT THE POLICE OFFICER SELECTION TESTS

Before this book presents you with sample police officer selection tests, here are a few important points to note about your time at the assessment centre.

When attending the assessment centre it will last approximately 5 hours. To take part in the assessment you must ensure you read all documentation clearly on your invite and bring all required documentation.

When attending the assessment centre you will be asked to bring certain documents to confirm your identity. You should check your specific application for exact requirements but normally these documents include:

A full 10 plus year passport or two of the following documents:

- British driver's licence
- P45
- Proof of address (For example, a water/gas/phone bill)
- Birth certificate - issued within 6 weeks of your birth
- Credit card with your photo on it
- Chequebook and your bank card - along with three statements and proof of signature.

It is very important that you bring proof of identity to the assessment centre otherwise you will not be allowed to take part.

If you have any concerns about your assessment you will be given the opportunity to ask questions and sort them out before your assessment begins.

Do not arrive late to your assessment as the assessment centre follows a strict timetable. You will not be allowed to take part if you arrive late.

***Tip** – Always behave professionally and appropriately between exercises, you are being assessed continuously.*

During your time at the assessment centre you will be assessed on:

- 4 interactive exercises
- 2 written exercises
- A competency based structured interview
- 2 psychometric tests

HOW YOU'RE ASSESSED

For these exercises you will be assessed by trained assessors on **what** you do and **how** you do it. Information from all the exercises will be used to determine whether or not you have demonstrated your ability to meet the national standard. Although this does not guarantee you will be successful in obtaining your post within the police force. Factors such as other candidates scoring higher than yourself or available vacancies can also determine your success.

TYPES OF TESTS

You will face 2 main types of psychometric tests at the assessment centre. A **numerical** ability test and a **verbal** ability test. Both tests are multiple choice questions that you will take in an exercise room along with other candidates.

Your results for the numerical and verbal reasoning tests will be assessed by converting your scores to a grade scale from A – D. The highest performing candidates will be awarded an A grade whilst candidates who do not perform so well will be awarded with a D grade.

SAMPLE TEST QUESTIONS

When preparing for the numerical and verbal reasoning tests the most effective way to increase your scores is to simply practise plenty of sample questions. Within this guide I have provided you with a number of sample test questions. In addition to these you may also decide to purchase additional testing resources. If you do decide to pursue this option then I recommend the following:

1. Numerical reasoning and verbal reasoning testing booklets from the website www.how2become.co.uk.

2. Consider practising online tests through the website www.job-test.co.uk.

I have now provided you with a number of practice sample questions that you may encounter during your tests. It is unlikely that you will be asked these exact questions during your assessment but please do use them as part of your preparation as they will be very similar to the actual tests.

Work as quickly as possible through each question and see how well you score. Try to understand each question and read it carefully. The answers to each question are at the end of the exercises.

During the verbal reasoning tests that follow, use a pen and paper and answer each question as TRUE, FALSE or IMPOSSIBLE TO SAY.

REMEMBER TO ANSWER YOUR QUESTIONS BASED SOLELY ON THE INFORMATION GIVEN AND NOT ON YOUR OWN OPINIONS OR VIEWS.

THE **TESTING** SERIES
POLICE **TESTS**

THE **TESTING** SERIES
expert advice on test preparation

Orders: Please contact How2become Ltd,
Suite 2, 50 Churchill Square Business Centre, Kings Hill, Kent ME19 4YU.

You can order via the email address info@how2become.co.uk or via our distributor Gardners.com.

ISBN: 978-1910202319

Printed in Great Britain for How2become Ltd by CMP (uk) Limited, Dorset.

INTRODUCTION
TO YOUR
NEW GUIDE

Welcome to Police Tests: The ULTIMATE guide for helping you pass the Police Initial Recruitment Test. This guide has been designed to help you prepare for, and pass the tough police officer selection process.

The selection process to join the police is highly competitive. Approximately 65,000 people apply to join the police every year. But what is even more staggering is that only approximately 7,000 of those applicants will be successful. You could view this as a worrying statistic, or alternatively you could view it that you are determined to be one of the 7,000 who are successful. Armed with this insider's guide, you have certainly taken the first step to passing the police officer selection process.

The guide itself has been split up into useful testing sections to make it easier for you to prepare for the PIRT. There are plenty of test questions for you to try out. Once you have completed the testing booklet you may wish to access our online police testing facility which you can find at:

WWW.HOW2BECOME.CO.UK

Don't ever give up on your dreams; if you really want to become a police officer then you can do it. The way to approach the police officer selection process is to embark on a programme of 'in depth' preparation and this guide will help you to do exactly that.

The police officer selection process is not easy to pass. Unless, that is, you put in plenty of preparation. Your preparation must be focused in the right areas, and also be comprehensive enough to give you every chance of success. This guide will teach you how to be a successful candidate.

The way to pass the police officer selection process is to develop your own skills and experiences around the core competencies that are required to become a police officer. Many candidates who apply to join the police will be unaware that the core competencies even exist. This guide has been specifically designed to help you prepare for the Police Initial Recruitment Test that forms part of the assessment centre. Towards the end of the guide you will also find a useful section dedicated to report writing, including sample report writing exercises for you to try.

If you need any further help with any element of the police officer selection process, including role play, written test and interview, then we offer a wide range of products to assist you. These are all available through our online shop www.how2become.co.uk. We also run a 1-day intensive Police Officer Course.

Details are available at the website:

WWW.POLICECOURSE.CO.UK

Once again, thank you for your custom and we wish you every success in your pursuit to becoming a police officer.

Work hard, stay focused and be what you want…

Best wishes,

Richard McMunn

VERBAL REASONING QUESTIONS
SECTION ONE

The verbal reasoning test is designed to measure your ability to read a written situation and make sense of it. The verbal reasoning test consists of **28 questions** and last for **30 minutes**.

The test is **split into two sections** (Section A and Section B). Section A has three possible answers where only one answer is correct. Section B has four possible answers where once again only one answer is correct.

SECTION A

In Section A of the verbal reasoning test you will be given a statement/ written situation in which you will be provided with multiple conclusions. You must decide if:

A – The conclusion is **true** based on the facts of the given situation.

B – The conclusion is **false** based on the facts of the given situation.

C – It is **impossible to say** based on the facts of the given situation.

SECTION B

As in Section A you will be provided with a written situation and multiple choice answers. This time you will be give four statements and it will be your task to assess each statement and decide which one best suites the information provided.

VERBAL REASONING QUESTION NUMBER 1

An accident occurred on the M6 motorway between junctions 8 and 9 southbound at 3pm. The driver of a Ford Fiesta was seen to pull into the middle lane without indicating, forcing another car to veer into the central reservation. One person suffered a broken arm and was taken to hospital before the police arrived.

A = TRUE **B** = FALSE **C** = IMPOSSIBLE TO SAY

1. The accident was on the M6 motorway on the carriageway that leads to Scotland.

2. The driver of the Ford Fiesta was injured in the crash.

3. The central reservation was responsible for the accident.

4. The police did not give first aid at the scene.

5. The accident happened at 1500 hours.

VERBAL REASONING QUESTION NUMBER 2

A man of between 30 and 35 years of age was seen stealing a car from outside Mrs Brown's house yesterday. He was seen breaking the nearside rear window with a hammer before driving off at 40 miles per hour. He narrowly missed a young mother who was pushing a pram.

A = TRUE **B** = FALSE **C** = IMPOSSIBLE TO SAY

1. The man who stole the car was 34 years old.

2. He stole Mrs Brown's car.

3. The young mother who was pushing a pram was injured.

4. He used a hammer to smash the windscreen.

5. When he drove off he was breaking the speed limit.

VERBAL REASONING QUESTION NUMBER 3

A shopkeeper called Mr Smith was seen serving alcohol to a girl aged 16.

The girl had shown him fake ID, which was a driving licence belonging to her sister. The incident occurred at around 11.30pm on a Wednesday evening during December.

A = TRUE   **B** = FALSE **C** = IMPOSSIBLE TO SAY

1. The girl is old enough to purchase alcohol from Mr Smith.

2. The girl purchased the alcohol for her sister.

3. The girl's sister had given the driving licence to her.

4. Mr Smith will receive a custodial sentence for his actions.

VERBAL REASONING QUESTION NUMBER 4

Following a bank robbery in a town centre, 6 masked gunmen were seen speeding away from the scene in a black van. The incident, which happened in broad daylight in front of hundreds of shoppers, was picked up by CCTV footage. Police are appealing for witnesses. The local newspaper has offered a £5,000 reward for any information leading to the conviction of all the people involved.

A = TRUE   **B** = FALSE **C** = IMPOSSIBLE TO SAY

1. The vehicle in which the gunmen drove off was a black van.

2. Someone must have seen something.

3. The incident was picked up by CCTV cameras.

4. The newspaper will pay £5,000 for information leading to the arrest of all of the men involved.

5. Police are not appealing to members of the public for help.

VERBAL REASONING QUESTION NUMBER 5

A factory fire at 'Stevenage Supplies' was arson, the police have confirmed. A man was seen running away from the scene shortly before the fire started. Earlier that day a man was sacked from the company for allegedly stealing money from the safe. The incident is the second one to occur at the factory in as many months.

A = TRUE **B** = FALSE **C** = IMPOSSIBLE TO SAY

1. Police have confirmed that the fire at the factory was arson.

2. The man who was seen running away from the fire was the man who started it.

3. One previous 'fire-related' incident has already occurred at the factory.

4. The man who was sacked from the factory may have started the fire.

VERBAL REASONING QUESTION NUMBER 6

At 1800 hours today police issued a statement in relation to the crime scene in Armstrong Road. Police have been examining the scene all day and reports suggest that it may be murder. Forensic officers have been visiting the incident and inform us that the whole street has been cordoned off and nobody will be allowed through. Police say that the street involved will be closed for another 18 hours and no access will be available to anyone during this time.

A = TRUE **B** = FALSE **C** = IMPOSSIBLE TO SAY

1. Police have confirmed the incident is murder.

2. Forensic officers have now left the scene.

3. The road will be open at 12 noon the following day.

4. Although the street has been cordoned off, taxis and buses will be given access.

5. Forensic officers will be at the scene all night.

VERBAL REASONING QUESTION NUMBER 7

Mrs Rogers telephoned the police at 8pm to report a burglary at her house in Gamble Crescent. She reports that she came home from work and her front bedroom window was open but she doesn't remember leaving it open.

She informs the police that her jewellery box is missing and also £40 cash, which was left on the kitchen table. She came home from work at 5pm and left again at 7am in the morning. No other signs of forced entry were visible.

A = TRUE   **B** = FALSE **C** = IMPOSSIBLE TO SAY

1. The burglar made his/her way in through the bedroom window.

2. The burglar took the jewellery and £40 cash before leaving.

3. Mrs Rogers was away from the house for 10 hours in total.

4. Mrs Rogers may have left the window open herself before leaving for work.

5. There were other visible signs of forced entry.

VERBAL REASONING QUESTION NUMBER 8

The local bank was held up at gunpoint on Monday the 18th of September at approximately 4pm. The thieves used a black motorcycle to make their getaway.

The following facts are also known about the incident:

- Two shots were fired.
- There were 12 staff members on duty at the time of the raid.
- The alarm was raised by the manager and the police were called.
- The cashier was ordered to hand over a bag of money containing £7,000.
- The thieves have not yet been caught.
- Police are appealing for witnesses.

A = TRUE   **B** = FALSE **C** = IMPOSSIBLE TO SAY

1. The thieves have been caught.

2. The cashier raised the alarm.

3. The cashier was shot.

4. Two people were injured.

5. The bank was open for business at the time of the incident.

VERBAL REASONING QUESTION NUMBER 9

A father and son were found dead in their two-bedroom flat in Sparsbrook on Sunday evening. They had both been suffocated.

The following facts are also known:

- The victims were identified by the police as Mark Webster, 16 years old, and his father, Thomas Webster, 39 years old.
- Thomas was in debt to the sum of £37,000.
- Two men were seen leaving the house at 4pm on Sunday afternoon.
- Two men were seen acting suspiciously in the area on Saturday evening before driving off in a Brown Ford Escort car.
- Thomas had previously contacted the police to express his concerns about his safety following threats from his creditors.
- The house had not been broken into.

A = TRUE   B = FALSE   C = IMPOSSIBLE TO SAY

1. The people Thomas owed money to could have been responsible for the deaths.
2. The two men seen leaving the house were not responsible for the deaths of Mark Webster and Thomas Webster.
3. The house had been broken into.
4. Neighbours reported two men acting suspiciously in the area on Saturday evening.
5. The people responsible for the deaths drove off in a brown Ford Escort car.

VERBAL REASONING QUESTION NUMBER 10

Firefighters have discovered a large quantity of cannabis during a fire on a farm in the village of Teynsville. Police have cordoned off the area.

The following facts are also known about the incident:

- The farm is owned by local farmer Peter Watts.
- The fire was deliberately started.
- Peter Watts has two previous convictions for possession and supply of Class A drugs.
- Peter Watts wife was at home on the night of the fire.
- Peter Watts was visiting friends in the nearby town of Grentshill when the fire started.
- A passer-by reported the fire to the police at 9pm.
- Peter Watts has been arrested on suspicion of possession of cannabis.

A = TRUE **B** = FALSE **C** = IMPOSSIBLE TO SAY

1. Cannabis is a Class A drug.

2. The fire was started accidentally.

3. A passer-by reported the fire to the fire service at 9pm.

4. The cannabis found during the fire belonged to Peter Watts.

5. Peter Watts has been arrested for possession of cannabis.

VERBAL REASONING QUESTION NUMBER 11

A row of terraced houses was partially destroyed by an explosion on the 17th of April 2007. Just before the explosion a man was seen running back into his house. He had reported a gas leak to the gas board 7 days prior to the explosion.

The following facts are also known about the incident:

- The smell of gas had also been reported by two further residents in the weeks leading up to the explosion.

- The police are investigating possible terrorist connections with one of the residents.

A = TRUE   **B** = FALSE **C** = IMPOSSIBLE TO SAY

1. A gas leak was reported to the gas board on the 10th of April 2007.

2. The explosion was caused by a gas leak.

3. The explosion was not caused by a terrorist attack.

4. The man seen running back into his house had already reported a gas leak to the gas board.

5. The row of terraced houses that were involved in the explosion has been damaged.

VERBAL REASONING QUESTION NUMBER 12

On the evening of December 21 Peterborough Boat Club was vandalised. The police are carrying out investigations.

The only facts known at this stage are:

- The boat club insurance had lapsed.
- The club Chairman was Nick Foster.
- Gary Newman owns a boat at the club.
- Gary Newman had fallen out with Nick Foster.
- Gary Newman was away on Holiday the week before Christmas.
- No boats were damaged.
- The Club house keys were found in Gary Newman's house.

A = TRUE   **B** = FALSE **C** = IMPOSSIBLE TO SAY

1. Nick Foster may have vandalised the boat club.

2. The Club will be able to claim on their insurance.

3. Gary Newman visited the boat club on December 21.

4. Nick Foster could have been at the boat club when the vandalism took place.

5. There are definite grounds to arrest Gary Newman for vandalism.

VERBAL REASONING QUESTION NUMBER 13

On July 28, the gym at King Edward Grammar School, in Smithfield, was burnt to the ground. Only the local Fire and Rescue service attended the scene at 21:00.

The only facts known at this stage are:

- A local teenager, John Hallam, was at the school at 20:00.
- John Hallam was expelled from school a fortnight ago for bad behaviour.
- The gym alarm was on.
- The fire was started using a petrol bomb.
- The ambulance service attended the scene at 21:30.
- A King Edward Grammar School pupil, Sally Jones, was admitted to hospital on July 28.

A = TRUE **B** = FALSE **C** = IMPOSSIBLE TO SAY

1. The Police and Fire and Rescue service attended the scene at 21:00.

2. John Hallam may have petrol bombed the gym.

3. John Hallam was expelled from King Edward Grammar School.

4. Sally Jones was injured in the fire.

5. The gym alarm may not have sounded when set off.

VERBAL REASONING QUESTION NUMBER 14

Tony Murphy was stabbed on the evening of October 17 in Upton Park, Sudbury. He later died in hospital from his injuries.

The only facts known at this stage are:

- He was stabbed in the heart
- Tony left a local pub near Upton Park at 7pm.
- A dead body was found in the Upton Park area at 10pm.
- Tony had visited a cash machine before entering the park.
- Tony was heavily drunk.
- Tony left his home for the pub at 2pm.

A = TRUE   **B** = FALSE **C** = IMPOSSIBLE TO SAY

1. Tony was drinking alcohol for 5 hours.

2. Tony's dead body was found in the park at 22:00hrs.

3. Tony may have been robbed and stabbed for money.

4. Tony was knifed in the heart.

5. Tony died from his injuries at the scene.

VERBAL REASONING QUESTION NUMBER 15

After 12-years of marriage, Jane Smith left her husband Tom Smith and moved to a different town.

The only facts known at this stage are:

- Tom cheated on Jane during their marriage.
- Jane wanted to move to Driffield.
- Jane and Tom have been divorced for two-years.
- Tom has a new partner called Sarah.
- Tom and Jane got married when they were twenty two.
- Tom and Sarah have a three-year-old child together.

A = TRUE **B** = FALSE **C** = IMPOSSIBLE TO SAY

1. Jane was 36 years old when she and Tom got divorced.

2. Tom and Jane have a three-year-old child together.

3. Tom slept with Sarah while he was still married to Jane.

4. Toms philandering was the reason for the divorce.

5. Jane left Tom and moved to Driffield.

VERBAL REASONING QUESTION NUMBER 16

On July 5 at 15:10 a light aircraft crash-landed in a field. There were two people inside the plane — one died from his injuries. The killed crash victim was identified as Ken Stone, an aviation enthusiast, from Retford.

The only facts known at this stage are:

- The aircraft took off from a local airfield at 2pm.
- An increase in bird activity was reported in the area surrounding the airfield.
- The nearest airfield to Retford is Gamston.
- A mayday call was heard at 15:05.
- Ken Stone visited the Gamston airfield every weekend.
- The crash occurred two-miles south of Waddington Airfield.

A = TRUE   **B** = FALSE **C** = IMPOSSIBLE TO SAY

1. Ken Stone was the pilot of the light aircraft.

2. The plane may have had a bird strike leading the crash.

3. The emergency occurred at 15:05.

4. The light aircraft was in the air for one-hour 20-minutes before it crashed.

5. The aircraft took off from Waddington Airfield.

VERBAL REASONING QUESTION NUMBER 17

A 53-year-old man was found dead near a lake by his car. A post-mortem examination was carried out on the body and it was found that the man died from a gunshot wound to his head.

The only facts known at this stage are:

- Melvin Jones' only daughter recently died in a car accident.
- Melvin Jones had life insurance worth £600,000.
- The man in the car was identified as Melvin Jones.
- Melvin Jones took the death of his daughter very badly.
- Caroline planned to divorce her husband.

A = TRUE   **B** = FALSE **C** = IMPOSSIBLE TO SAY

1. Melvin Jones might have committed suicide.

2. Melvin Jones was murdered.

3. Melvin Jones could not face life without his daughter.

4. Caroline planned to kill Melvin for the insurance money.

5. Melvin has had only one child.

VERBAL REASONING QUESTION NUMBER 18

A lorry depot was broken into between 11:00pm and 04:00am. The night guard was on duty between 09:00pm and 03:00am. It was discovered that the depot had been broken into at 04:00am. A window was found broken on the south side of the building.

The only facts known at this stage are:

- The night guard reported no problems while on duty.
- A local resident saw a man acting suspiciously around the depot at 12:15pm.
- The depot stored high priced electronics.
- The depot had repeatedly reported lost stock items.
- The robbery occurred on Saturday morning.
- There was no CCTV evidence.

A = TRUE   **B** = FALSE **C** = IMPOSSIBLE TO SAY

1. A suspicious woman was seen around the depot at 12:15pm.

2. The thief broke in through a window on the north side of the building.

3. The break in occurred between 03:00am and 04:00am on Saturday.

4. The CCTV evidence may have been removed from the depot.

5. Windows may be broken on the north side of the building.

VERBAL REASONING QUESTION NUMBER 19

At 01:45am door staff ejected two drunken men from a nightclub. At 02:30am two members of door staff were seriously assaulted, resulting in both of them being admitted to hospital. One man is in a stable condition while the other is in a critical condition, undergoing immediate surgery. These were the only door staff admitted to the hospital during the early hours of the morning.

The only facts known at this stage are:

- Door staff ejected Ben Shamrock and Rob Holmes from a nightclub.
- Ben Shamrock had previous convictions for assault.
- Dave Meadows was admitted to hospital with a stab wound to his chest.
- Dave Meadows and Tim Smith work for Wildcat nightclub as doormen.
- Ben Shamrock stabbed Dave Meadows in the chest.
- Tim Smith was admitted to hospital following an assault- he remains in a stable condition.
- Tim Smith only works on a Friday night.

A = TRUE   B = FALSE C = IMPOSSIBLE TO SAY

1. Ben Shamrock stabbed Dave Meadows in the chest.

2. Dave Meadows had to undergo immediate surgery.

3. The assault occurred outside Wildcat nightclub.

4. Ben Shamrock and Rob Holmes were ejected from the Wildcat nightclub prior to the offence.

5. The assault occurred on a Saturday night at 02:30am.

VERBAL REASONING QUESTION NUMBER 20

On Sunday, December 7, Police Traffic Officers attended a fatal road traffic incident. The Police were at the scene of the incident from 2:10am. There were two male passengers and one female passenger in a car. There was one fatality in the collision.

The only facts known at this stage are:

- Jamie Matlock is the owner of the vehicle.
- Jamie was out drinking in a nightclub from 21:00 Saturday until 02:00 Sunday.
- Jamie has a girlfriend called Karen Miller.
- A female from the accident was pronounced dead at hospital.
- Jamie's best friend Tom Anderson has previous drink driving convictions.
- The driver of the vehicle was not insured.
- No pedestrians were involved.

A = TRUE   **B** = FALSE **C** = IMPOSSIBLE TO SAY

1. Jamie Matlock was the driver of the vehicle.

2. A pedestrian may have been killed.

3. Karen Miller died in the accident.

4. Jamie drove his vehicle to the nightclub at 21:30.

5. Tom Anderson was driving the vehicle under the influence of alcohol.

6. Jamie Matlock, Karen Miller and Tom Anderson may not have been involved in the accident.

VERBAL REASONING QUESTION NUMBER 21

On Saturday, May 7, a school caretaker found a number of broken windows on the north side of the school building. A local teenager was seen on a CCTV camera loitering in the vicinity of the school. He was recorded later leaving the area. He was identified as Graham Smyth.

The only facts known at this stage are:

- Graham Smyth once attended Melton Grammar School.
- The caretaker works from 08:00 until 14:00 on a Saturday.
- There were no broken windows when the caretaker locked up on Friday evening at 18:00.
- Local teenagers play golf on the pitches towards the north of the school.
- Graham Smyth had recently been expelled from The Melton School.
- The school only has CCTV on the south side of the building.
- The caretaker works for Melton Grammar School.

A = TRUE **B** = FALSE **C** = IMPOSSIBLE TO SAY

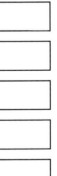

1. The windows were broken between the hours of 18:00 Friday and 08:00 Saturday.

2. Graham Smyth may have broken the windows in a revenge attack for being expelled from the school.

3. CCTV could have recorded the windows being broken.

4. Golf balls could have broken the windows.

5. Graham Smyth was playing golf.

VERBAL REASONING QUESTION NUMBER 22

The Southton Police Incident Response Team (IRT) was called to a domestic violence incident on a Saturday evening at approximately 22:00. On arrival they discovered a female who had been seriously assaulted. A male was arrested and later charged with assault. His mother, the homeowner, called the police.

The only facts known at this stage are:

- The victim had repeatedly been assaulted by her brother Ross Jones.
- The Police IRT consists of two officers.
- Police attended one domestic violence call on Saturday night at 2 Clermont Drive.
- Katherine Jones is the owner of 2 Clermont Drive.
- Katherine Jones' daughter Sara Dolby was staying over that night.

A = TRUE **B** = FALSE **C** = IMPOSSIBLE TO SAY

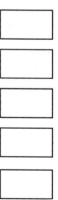

1. Ross Jones assaulted the female on Saturday night.

2. The assault happened on Saturday at 22:00.

3. Katherine Jones was the female assaulted.

4. A single Police Officer attended the scene.

5. Katherine Jones called the Police on Saturday at 10:00am.

6. Sara Dolby was not a repeat victim.

VERBAL REASONING QUESTION NUMBER 23

A young child disappeared from a local food shop in Kinston after her mother became distracted at the counter. The mother asked the shop assistant to ring Kinston Police when she discovered her child had disappeared. The police arrived 10-minutes after they were called. Another shopper reported seeing the child being walked away from the shop by a male who was approximately 6-ft tall, with brown hair.

The only facts known at this stage are:

- The mother Miss Jenkins has red hair.
- Police were called at 10:25am on Saturday morning.
- Miss Jenkins had just spoken to her child's father 10-minutes prior to her disappearance.
- The child's name is Molly.
- Molly's father has brown hair and is approximately 5 ft 11.
- Tony Woods has a child with Miss Jenkins.

A = TRUE   **B** = FALSE **C** = IMPOSSIBLE TO SAY

1. The Police arrived on the scene at 10.25am Saturday morning.

2. Tony Woods is Molly's father.

3. Molly's father may have taken her.

4. Molly disappeared from a food shop in Kinston.

5. Molly must have red or brown hair.

VERBAL REASONING QUESTION NUMBER 24

During the summer Mrs Olds called Neslington County Council on 12 occasions reporting anti-social behaviour. Twenty-five-per-cent of the calls were about local drunk Andy Young loitering and discarding empty beer cans in her garden. Half of all the calls were because local teenagers were causing a nuisance around her semi-detached house, including disturbing behaviour and criminal damage. Mrs Olds reported that she felt scared in her own home.

The only facts known at this stage are:

- Local teenagers have been stopped by police and found with alcohol near Mrs Olds property.
- Two calls were because next door neighbours were playing music too loud.
- The Ford family live next door to Mr and Mrs Olds.
- Mrs Olds' husband is retired.
- Mrs Olds lives next to a park were teenager frequent.
- A neighbour, Mr Cook, has been warned about playing music too loud.

A = TRUE   **B** = FALSE **C** = IMPOSSIBLE TO SAY

1. Mrs Olds called the council three times about Andy Young.

2. Mrs Olds is retired.

3. Mrs Olds reported Mr Cook twice for playing his music too loud.

4. The park is possibly a reason the anti-social behaviour occurs.

5. Alcohol is the main cause of the anti-social behaviour.

VERBAL REASONING QUESTION NUMBER 25

A kebab shop in Shrewsbury has had bricks and rocks thrown at its windows and doors on more than five separate occasions. The owner believes it to be race-related and has told the police that he thinks the latest incident was a local teenager called Louise Murphy. The incidents always occur between 22:00 and 24:00.

The only facts known at this stage are:

- Police know that Louis Murphy is subject to a tagging order.
- The owner of the shop is Malik Ahkmed.
- Louis cannot leave his house between the hours of 19:00 and 07:00.
- Malik Ahkmed has recently had an argument with another local kebab shop owner Stelios Romis.
- Stelios Romis employs a 17-year-girl old called Louise.
- Louise had prevsiously worked for Malik.
- The Police have only received three reports of windows and doors being broken by rocks and bricks being thrown at Malik's kebab shop (The Kebab House).

A = TRUE   **B** = FALSE **C** = IMPOSSIBLE TO SAY

1. Malik's kebab shop's windows have been smashed repeatedly.

2. Louis Murphy may have thrown the bricks through the window.

3. Bricks and rocks were the only objects thrown.

4. Malik and Stelios had an argument about Louise.

5. Police were called after every incident.

6. The incident happened because Malik is a Muslim.

7. The Kebab House has had more than five incidents of bricks and rocks being thrown at its windows.

VERBAL REASONING QUESTION NUMBER 26

During the evening of July, 8, number 88 Victoria Street, Grimley, was set on fire. The police are treating the fire as suspicious.

The only facts known at this stage are:

- Sarah Williams owns the house.
- The occupants had recently taken out insurance.
- A neighbour, Katie Forester, was known to dislike Miss Williams.
- Between July 8 and July 15, Mrs Forester was away on holiday in Spain
- No one died in the blaze.
- A Mrs Williams had been recorded buying petrol from a local petrol station on July 8.

A = TRUE **B** = FALSE **C** = IMPOSSIBLE TO SAY

1. Sarah Williams died in the blaze.

2. Katie Forester may have started the blaze.

3. Miss Williams was recorded buying petrol from a local petrol station on July 8.

4. Katie Forester lives at 87 Victoria Street.

5. Miss Williams may have started the blaze to benefit from an insurance claim.

VERBAL REASONING QUESTION NUMBER 27

A Police traffic unit pulled over a suspected drink driver because his driving was erratic. The driver said he had been to a house party and had only had one can of beer.

The only facts known at this stage are:

- The car was a five-door estate.
- The car had three occupants.
- Two of the occupants admitted having had consumed alcohol.
- James Culshaw was the driver.
- The driver failed the road side breath test.
- The party was less than one-mile from the location where Mr Culshaw was stopped.

A = TRUE   B = FALSE **C** = IMPOSSIBLE TO SAY

1. Mr Culshaw told the Police he had not consumed any alcohol that night.

2. Mr Culshaw had more than one can of beer.

3. The passengers were also drunk.

4. Mr Culshaw was pulled over because he didn't have his lights on.

5. Mr Culshaw had a full car load.

VERBAL REASONING QUESTION NUMBER 28

Mr Rawlings lives on Sutcliffe Drive. On November 3, Mr Rawling had a firework put through the letterbox of his bungalow. This set the house on fire. Mr Rawlings was assisted out his house by his neighbours, Mr Hawkins and Mr Jenkins. Two fire appliances attended and it took 32-minutes to extinguish the flames. A teenager rang 999 to report the fire. Teenagers were seen loitering close to Mr Rawlings house.

The only facts known at this stage are:

- Mr Rawlings had recently been in court as a witness against a local teenager, Tyrone Mills.
- Mr Rawlings is elderly and finds it difficult to walk or climb stairs.
- Mr Rawlings has reported anti-social behaviour around his house to police.
- It took the fire service six- minutes to attend the call.
- Mr Rawlings lives on his own but does have family who visit.
- The firework was put through his door at 20:35.
- The teenager called the emergency services at 20:45.

A = TRUE **B** = FALSE **C** = IMPOSSIBLE TO SAY

1. The fire was extinguished between 21:20 and 21:30.

2. The firework was payback for Mr Rawlings going to court.

3. Mr Rawlings may have been upstairs when the fire started.

4. Mr Rawlings neighbours, Mrs Hawkins and Mrs Jenkins, helped him out his house.

5. It took one fire engine 32 minutes to extinguish the fire.

VERBAL REASONING QUESTION NUMBER 29

This morning at 6am Shepham Police raided a property with a warrant to search it for drugs. They found a selection of items commonly used to grow cannabis and a number of small cannabis plants. Police are still searching the property.

The latest reported facts are:

- The house is owned by Amanda Holder.
- She lives in the property with her partner, Michael Smith and his son, James Smith.
- Amanda and James do not get along.
- Michael works on an oil rig and has been away from home for two months.
- The drug growing equipment was found in James' room.
- All three have previous convictions for possessing drugs.

A = TRUE **B** = FALSE **C** = IMPOSSIBLE TO SAY

1. Amanda Holder has been convicted of producing drugs before.

2. The door of the house was damaged in the drug raid.

3. Michael may not be aware of the drugs.

4. James may have been growing the drugs to spite Amanda.

5. Michael may have planted the cannabis plants a month ago.

VERBAL REASONING QUESTION NUMBER 30

As part of a summer drink driving clampdown Doggington Police are stopping drivers randomly and asking them to provide voluntary breath samples.

The only facts known about the campaign so far are:

- On the first night 65 drivers agreed to provide samples.
- One of them was over the legal drink-drive limit.
- Sarah Newman had been drinking in the pub all day after splitting up with her partner.
- Police asked her to provide a sample after she hit a kerb while driving.
- She failed the roadside breath test and was taken into custody until she sobered up.
- The car she was driving belonged to her partner

A = TRUE   **B** = FALSE **C** = IMPOSSIBLE TO SAY

1. Sarah Newman was not insured to drive the car.

2. She damaged the wheel of the car when she drove it into the kerb.

3. Sarah Newman failed to provide a breath sample at the road side.

4. Sarah Newman was the only driver to fail the roadside breath test on the first night of the campaign.

5. She has been arrested for drink driving.

VERBAL REASONING QUESTION NUMBER 31

Jeff Bridges claims he has had his garden shed broken into. A crow bar was found in the garden and the door of the shed had been forced open using it. Mr Bridges claims that a lawn mower, a strimmer, a new spade and a garden fork have been stolen. He says that last week a group of young people graffitied the side wall of his house and he thinks they are to blame. The ringleader of the gang, Sam Smith has recently started a gardening company.

The latest reported facts are:

- Sam Smith had previous convictions for breaking and entering.
- Sam Smith has a variety of new gardening equipment for his company — including a spade the same as Mr Bridges.
- Mr Bridges spade was bought from popular high street shop B & P.
- Mr Bridges claims the items stolen were worth £400.
- Mr Bridges says Sam Smith has been harassing him
- Sam Smith's dad fired Mr Bridges from his marketing company last month.

A = TRUE   **B** = FALSE **C** = IMPOSSIBLE TO SAY

1. Mr Bridges had a grudge against Sam Smith.

2. The items stolen from Mr Bridges shed are worth more than £400.

3. Sam Smith may have stolen Mr Bridges spade.

4. The crow bar found in Mr Bridges garden was used to force open the shed.

5. Police may find Sam Smith's fingerprints at the scene.

VERBAL REASONING QUESTION NUMBER 32

A fire has occurred in a nightclub belonging to Harry James. One person died in the fire, which occurred at 11pm on Saturday night. The club was insured for less than its value.

A = TRUE   **B** = FALSE **C** = IMPOSSIBLE TO SAY

1. The fire occurred at 1100 hours.

2. A relative of Harry James was killed in the fire.

3. If the insurance company decide to pay out for the fire, Harry James stands to make a profit.

4. The fire was caused by arson.

5. The club was not insured at the time of the fire.

ANSWERS TO VERBAL REASONING QUESTIONS — SECTION 1

Question 1

1.   False

2.   Impossible to say

3.   False

4.   True

5.   True

Question 2

1.   Impossible to say

2.   Impossible to say

3.   False

4.   False

5.   Impossible to say

Question 3

1.   False

2.   Impossible to say

3.   Impossible to say

4.   Impossible to say

Question 4

1.   True

2.   Impossible to say

3.   True

4.   False

5.   False

Question 5

1. True

2. Impossible to say

3. True

4. True

Question 6

1. False

2. Impossible to say

3. True

4. False

5. Impossible to say

Question 7

1. Impossible to say

2. Impossible to say

3. False

4. True

5. False

Question 8

1. False.

2. False.

3. Impossible to say.

4. Impossible to say.

5. Impossible to say.

Question 9

1. True.

2. Impossible to say.

3. False.

4. Impossible to say.

5. Impossible to say.

Question 10

1. Impossible to say.

2. False.

3. False.

4. Impossible to say.

5. False.

Question 11

1. True.

2. Impossible to say.

3. Impossible to say.

4. True.

5. True.

Question 12

1. True.

2. False

3. Impossible to say.

4. Impossible to say.

5. False

Question 13

1. False.

2. True.

3. Impossible to say.

4. Impossible to say.

5. Impossible to say.

Question 14

1. Impossible to say.

2. False

3. True

4. Impossible to say.

5. False

Question 15

1. False

2. False

3. Impossible to say

4. Impossible to say

5. Impossible to say

Question 16

1. Impossible to say

2. True

3. True

4. False

5. Impossible to say

Question 17

1. True
2. Impossible to say
3. Impossible to say
4. Impossible to say
5. Impossible to say

Question 18

1. False
2. Impossible to say
3. Impossible to say
4. True
5. True

Question 19

1. True
2. True
3. Impossible to say
4. Impossible to say
5. False

Question 20

1. Impossible to say
2. False
3. Impossible to say
4. False
5. Impossible to say
6. True

Question 21

1. True
2. True
3. False
4. True
5. Impossible to say

Question 22

1. True
2. Impossible to say
3. False
4. False
5. False
6. Impossible to say

Question 23

1. False
2. Impossible to say
3. True
4. True
5. False

Question 24

1. True
2. Impossible to say
3. Impossible to say
4. True
5. Impossible to say

Question 25

1. True
2. False
3. Impossible to say
4. Impossible to say
5. False
6. Impossible to say
7. True

Question 26

1. False
2. True
3. False
4. Impossible to say
5. True

Question 27

1. False
2. Impossible to say
3. Impossible to say
4. False
5. False

Question 28

1. True
2. Impossible to say
3. False
4. False
5. False

Question 29

1. Impossible to say

2. Impossible to say

3. True

4. True

5. False

Question 30

1. Impossible to say

2. Impossible to say

3. False

4. True

5. Impossible to say

Question 31

1. Impossible to say

2. Impossible to say

3. True

4. True

5. True

Question 32

1. False

2. Impossible to say

3. False

4. Impossible to say

5. False

TIPS FOR PASSING THE VERBAL REASONING TEST

- In the build up to the assessment, make sure you practise plenty of sample test questions. Little and often is far more effective than cramming the night before your assessment.

- Read the questions carefully. During the test you may have to answer questions that are answered either TRUE, FALSE, or IMPOSSIBLE TO SAY. Base your answers on the evidence supplied only and not on your own views or opinions.

- Do not spend too long on one particular question. If you cannot answer it then move on to the next question but make sure you leave a space on the answer sheet.

- Consider purchasing additional verbal reasoning test booklets or practice aids. You can obtain these through the website www. how2become.co.uk.

- Get plenty of sleep the night before the test. This will allow you to concentrate fully.

VERBAL REASONING QUESTIONS
SECTION TWO

You must tick the answer which best matches the written situation.

QUESTION 1

At 1630 hours, Constable Robert Nixon interviewed a young boy who was arrested last night. At approximately 2100 hours the night before, a woman, whose name remains anonymous calls the police to tell them that she just witnessed two young boys coming out of a club in Maidstone, and got into a black Vauxhall corsa and drove off. She described the two young boys as being 18-19, and highly intoxicated.

The police sent out two patrol cars to the area in which the woman described. However, the woman did not take note of the number plate, nor did she know what they really looked like. The only useful information she gave was that they were 18-19, both had dark hair and both quite tall.

20 minutes later from the incident being reported, another call was made in regards to a black Vauxhall Corsa and that they had crashed into a tree on a country lane just on the outskirts of Maidstone Town Centre. The man who witness the crash, Tom Miles, gave a detailed description of the two young boys, and the police had no doubt that they were the same two boys as the anonymous woman had tried describing earlier.

A. Two people witnessed the young boys crash on the outskirts of Maidstone.

B. CCTV showed two boys crash into a tree in Maidstone.

C. The police received two phone calls regarding two young boys who seemed to be speaking about the same people.

D. The anonymous female witnessed the young boys crash into the tree.

QUESTION 2

PC Robert Harris was looking through CCTV in regards to a murder of a young local girl from Southampton. The local girl, Mia Tyler was found in a secluded wooded area just off a footpath near her home.

The last moments of Mia on CCTV is 90 minutes before her body was found. At 2130 hours, Mia was caught on CCTV in her local shops about 10 minutes from her house. The police have a 90 minute time gap from the last time she was seen on CCTV until the moments of her death.

Two weeks into the investigation, the Police finally have a lead. A young girl, aged 16 was also in the woods that night walking her dog with her mum and dad. She came across a bag, an identical one to the one Mia was supposedly missing when her body was found. The young girl stated that she did not see or hear anything strange, nothing out of the ordinary.

The police took the bag for forensic DNA testing in hope to find some answers. A breakthrough happened into the investigation, when the Police found fingerprints on the bag of Mia. These fingerprints were not hers, nor were they her families. In fact, the fingerprint belonged to the man who owned the local shop.

Her family said they had known the shop owner for a very long time and would be the last person to hurt their beloved Mia.

A. CCTV caught Mia at the local shops an hour before her body was found. ☐

B. The missing bag a young girl finds and the fingerprints the police trace lead them to the local shop owner. ☐

C. Mia's body was found by the local shop owner. ☐

D. The fingerprints on the bag was from one of her family members. ☐

QUESTION 3

At 08.30 this morning Constable Walker gathered CCTV footage from the High Street to Gabriel's Hill in Maidstone, Kent. He reviewed the CCTV of a stabbing that took place at 2145 hours the night before. He observed two adolescent boys wearing hooded tops walk over to a group of 4 young men. They stood facing one another, irritated and anger, shouting was apparent from watching the footage. The time recorded on the footage was 2155. The men stood facing one another, the CCTV only catching a glimpse of their side profiles. There a dozen people standing around watching the argument.

At 22.05 the two boys, who were wearing the hooded tops, threw the first punch to one of the four guys. The whole group go to defend him and they all start punching and fighting. At 22.17 one of the guys in the hooded top kneels down in pain, and by doing so, gives a guy from the opposing group to pull out a small object, and stabs him in the leg. At this time the group of 4 guys run off. The two guys wearing hooded tops are left on the floor, one bleeding from the leg and the other bleeding from the nose.

At 0915 in the interview room the next morning, the guy who pulled out the small object was being questioned. The small object he had was a pocket knife. He told the police that he was provoked, and that the guy who came over (the one who was stabbed in the leg) had been sleeping with his girlfriend. The young adolescent was put on bail but had to come back to attend a court hearing regarding his punishment.

A. The group of 4 young boys walked over to the two boys who were wearing hooded tops. ☐

B. 6 boys get in to a heated fight and was caught on CCTV. One of the boys stabs a boy in the leg with a pocket knife and 4 of them make a run for it. ☐

C. Two of the boys get stabbed and one person gets charged with causing bodily harm from using a knife. ☐

D. There is no CCTV to back up the story that a young boy gets stabbed in the leg during a fight. ☐

QUESTION 4

At 2130 hours it was dark. The street lights lit up the small neighbourhood of Privet Drive. The fog made it difficult to see clearly. PC Walker was walking down the street of the neighbourhood after he received a call that someone had been broken into. On his arrival, he noticed a distant shadow about 100 yards away from him, as he came closer, the shadow was a person, a teenage boy. The police officer stood quietly talking to the boy, general conversation that was all. The teenage boy had sandy blonde hair, blue eyes, and had a distinctive mole on his left cheek. He was wearing a smart pair of trousers and a polo shirt, and told the officer he was just on his way home from work.

The police officer left the boy and entered No.17, the house that had been broken into. He met the owner of the house in the living room, laying out a plate of biscuits and pouring a cup of tea. Mr David Brown was the owner of house for over 30 years, and claimed that he had never known anything like this to happen in this village.

PC Walker took a look around the house to gather up evidence. He decided to start the investigation upstairs, and as he got to the top of the stairs, he noticed the house had been turned inside out. As if someone had been looking for something. PC Walker asked the owner if he had any pride possessions or anything valuable that could of lead someone to break in and take it. David Brown, looked to floor and quietly whispered, "I had a gun, I've never used it. It was always a safety precaution ever since my late wife Camilla passed away".

PC Walker radioed the station to send out more patrol cars. When asked if he knew anyone that would of taken the gun, David said "no!". Meanwhile, as a few minutes passed, PC Walker came to an assumption. What if the boy he met early on in the night had something to do with it?

Back at the station, other police officers looked at the CCTV of the neighbourhood of Privet Drive. It did not show anything for a good hour or so, and then, in the corner of the screen, they noticed something. A shadow, about 100 yards away from the scene of the crime. The police analysed this further and zoomed in to the shadow, which resembled a person.

A. The teenage boy with sandy blonde hair was caught breaking into David Brown's house. ☐

B. CCTV caught the teenage boy breaking into the house. ☐

C. PC Walker witnessed the boy breaking into the house. ☐

D. CCTV caught the boy about 100 yards away from where the incident took place. ☐

QUESTION 5

An investigation into a murder was the main focus of a team at Kent Police Station. They had been gathering information and statements for the last 3 days on the death of 24 year old Mollie Richardson.

On the 13th April, 2014, Mollie Richardson's body was discovered in her family home in Kent. Her body was discovered by her boyfriend who was coming back from work away up north. He walked in through the back door and discovered her body in the living room. Mollie had several stab wounds to the abdomen and a severe gash on the left side of her head.

When the police and the forensic team went to investigate the scene of the crime, they found 3 vital pieces of evidence. Firstly, an obscure hand print was discovered on the side of the door that led to the hallway. This hand print belonged to her mother, Clarissa, who had recently gone away for the weekend with her new boyfriend. The second piece of evidence was an item of clothing that Mollie was wearing. The top that she was wearing had the DNA that had been matched up to the DNA of Mollie's mother's boyfriend, Dan Taylor. Thirdly, the position of her body in the living room was said to of been moved there from the kitchen, where the forensic team believed the incident took place. Due to the footprints of her boyfriend walking in and finding her as he left the kitchen, the police had to question his whereabouts.

Three pieces of evidence linked three different people to the scene of the crime.

A. Mollie's mother Clarissa was the prime suspect due to the blood stained hand print that was discovered. ☐

B. Mollie's boyfriend was the prime suspect due to his footprints leading from the kitchen into the living room at the place where Mollie's body was discovered. ☐

C. Mollie's mother's boyfriend was the prime suspect because of the DNA that matched his that was found on the top that Mollie was wearing at the time of her death. ☐

D. The police need more evidence before they can identify the person who killed Mollie. ☐

QUESTION 6

It was a busy afternoon on Saturday 3rd May, 2014 in the shopping centre at Lakeside. It was a hot day, and everyone was out enjoying the sunshine.

At approximately 1330 hours, a security guard from a high- end retail shop chased two boys out of the shop and through the shopping centre. The two boys, who were roughly 18 years old were stopped at the other end of the shopping centre by another security guard who received a message by his radio regarding this incident.

The two boys were took into a room and awaited for the police to arrive. Once the police arrived, the security guard that chased them down the shopping centre, Dan Baines, said that they had stolen a hat from the shop.

One of the boys, who was wearing the hat claimed he had it on the whole time and that he did not steal it. He stated "I entered the shop with the hat, I didn't steal it!". The other boy backed up his story.

The police were doubtful. They had statements from two boys against a security guard that has been working there for over 25 years.

As the boys became persistently agitated, the room got heated, and one of the boys went to lunge at the security guard.

The police officers escorted them all out of the room, through the shop to head towards the police car.

Meanwhile, assistant manager, Sandra Baker, walked over to them and asked if there was a problem. The security guard told her that the boys had stolen the hat from the shop. Sandra, looked at the hat and asked if that was the hat in question. "Yes".

Sandra looked from the boys to the police officers and stated "But these boys were wearing this hat when they came in"

A. The security guard witnessed the boys steal the hat from the shop and the shop assistant backed him up. ☐

B. No one saw the boys take anything, but Sandra did see the boys wearing the hat when they came in. ☐

C. The police officers arrested the boys because they had stolen the hat. ☐

D. There were 2 witnesses of the boys stealing a hat. ☐

QUESTION 7

At 10.30 this morning, Constable Davis collected the CCTV footage from the Londis shop on Heath Road. He reviewed the CCTV footage of a robbery that took place at 14.30 yesterday afternoon. Whilst watching the footage he observed two men, wearing black balaclavas), enter the shop through the main entrance. The time recorded on the footage was 21.35. The men walked towards the middle aisle and browsed the shelves, with only their backs to the CCTV camera. Four other people were in the shop, three customers and a female sales assistant. The customers were a man and two women.

At 21.47 the two female customers left the shop after paying for some alcohol and cigarettes. The other customer paid for a bottle of red wine and left the shop at 22.51. At 22.the taller man in the balaclava approached the counter. At this time the other man wearing the balaclava stood guard at the front entrance. The man took a hand gun from his jacket pocket and pointed it directly at the sales assistant. The sales assistant appeared to open the till and then the man seemed to pass a bag over the counter.

At 21.56 the sales assistant started filling the bag. Constable Davis then observed the main entrance shop door open with a man entering. The guy who was stood guard let him walk in and attacked him from behind. He pulled out a knife and stabbed the innocent man in the leg. The man fell to the ground, pleading with the men not to hurt the sales assistant. The two guys in balaclavas grabbed the bag and ran from the shop.

A. The shop was robbed by two men in balaclavas in the early hours of the morning. ☐

B. Two men in balaclavas stabbed the shop assistant in the leg and took the money from the counter. ☐

C. CCTV footage shows two men in balaclavas committing robbery in the shop with five witnesses. ☐

D. Only the female assistant and the guy who walked in later saw the two men in hoodies robbing the shop. ☐

QUESTION 8

At approximately 2030 hours, CCTV was being looked over at the local Police station regarding vandalism down at the local common, just under the South Gate Bridge.

CCTV from the 8th of March, shows a group of teenagers committing vandalism under the South Gate Bridge at 2130 hours. One of the teenagers, who spray painted the walls of the bridge was wearing a long white sleeved top, a body warmer, and white Nike trainers. The police wanted to find the group of teenagers to give them a warning regarding graffiti and vandalism on public property.

The CCTV was unclear and did not provide much help in trying to track down this group of young adolescents. However, a phone call later that afternoon proved useful. A woman claimed that as she was walking along the river of South Gate, on the other side of the bridge, she noticed the group of young teenagers vandalising. She recognised a couple of them, because of the close-knit neighbourhood that they shared and so she gave the police their details.

The police gave a caution to the group of teenagers and stated that "any more incidents like this and we will have to take further caution".

A. CCTV picked up the identities of the teenagers involved in the vandalising process. ☐

B. The identities of the teenagers were given by a woman who saw what was happening and knew who they were. ☐

C. The group of teenagers vandalised the local common and bridge in the early hours of the morning. ☐

D. CCTV caught the boy about 100 yards away from where the There were 2 witnesses of the group of teenagers vandalising. ☐

QUESTION 9

On the streets of Willington Street, at approximately 2100 hours, the ambulance arrived at the scene of a car accident.

There were 3 cars and 6 people involved in the accident. 3 men, 2 women and an 11 month old girl.

A red Vauxhall corsa had spun off the road, and was lying on its left side in a ditch. The other two cars, a black Ford Fiesta and silver Toyota Yaris were on the right side of the road facing each other. Both cars had a huge dent on the right side of the bonnet, windscreens smashed and the door of the Ford Fiesta was shattered and unable to open.

A statement given by the man driving the Ford stated that the Vauxhall was heading towards him and skidded into him. The next thing he knew was his car was spun round and hit the Toyota that was following behind the Vauxhall.

The statement given by the Vauxhall that he spotted something in the road and swerved to miss it. The Ford was doing a minimum of at least 40 around a sharp bend, which is why he hit the car and crashed into the ditch.

The woman driving the Toyota claimed that it was the Ford driver's fault for not looking at the sheer speed he was driving at. Although she stated that she did not see anything in the road that the Vauxhall tried to swerve from, if that was true the Vauxhall did the right thing.

A. It was driver of the Vauxhall's fault for swerving into the other side of the road and crashing into the Ford.

B. It was the driver of the Ford's fault for not reducing his speed around the corner and could of pretended the accident from happening.

C. The fact that everyone's story is different, it therefore makes it difficult to determine whose fault it was.

D. It was the Toyota's fault for driving too close to the Vauxhall in front which made him crash.

QUESTION 10

A call to Kent police station was made in regards to a hostage in a bank on the local high street. The Bank of HSBC was supposedly being held hostage by 2 men and a woman. It was approximately 16.30 when the police received the call.

As the police got in position outside the bank, they took their time inspecting and regulating the protocol of the upcoming action.

It was said that there was 12 staff on duty and over 10 customers inside the building the moment the building was took hostage.

At 17.05, what appeared to be a gun shot went off. Screams from inside the building echoed onto the streets. The police took a call from the woman who was holding them hostage. "If anyone comes anywhere near the building we start shooting".

The police played a strategic plan in order to prevent anything from happening. But they were running out of options and they were running out of time. The street was becoming darker, with the sudden rainfall falling heavily.

The incident finally come to an end when the police invaded the building, and took the chance of nothing would happen to the hostages.

Everyone was accounted for outside. A guy had been shot in the leg for resisting being taken hostage, but everyone else was not hurt. The only people not to be accounted for was a customer, and one of the guys who took them hostage in the first place.

After the police searching the building, it became apparent that the customer and the guy was nowhere to be seen in the building, nor the money that was taken from the cashiers.

A. Everyone escaped the bank without being hurt.   ☐

B. Everyone escaped the bank.   ☐

C. A customer and a guy who took them hostage had run off with the money that was taken from the bank.   ☐

D. All three people who took them hostage left the bank with the money.   ☐

ANSWERS TO VERBAL REASONING QUESTIONS – SECTION 2

Q1. C

Q2. B

Q3. B

Q4. D

Q5. D

Q6. B

Q7. D

Q8. B

Q9. C

Q10. C

NUMERICAL REASONING QUESTIONS

As part of the police tests you will also have to sit a numeracy assessment.

The most effective way to prepare for this type of test is to practise sample numerical reasoning tests.

Apart from the sample questions contained within this guide, there are a number of alternative methods for improving your scores. You may wish to invest in a psychometric numerical reasoning test booklet so that you can practise more tests. You can obtain more sample tests through the website www.how2become.co.uk.

The more you practise the better you will become at answering these types of questions.

Remember — practice makes perfect!

For the numerical reasoning test you will be asked to analyse numerical questions involving graphs, tables, charts and other numeracy questions. It is a multiple choice test that will require you to demonstrate your ability to use:

- Percentages
- Averages (mean)
- Ratios
- Addition

- Subtraction
- Multiplication
- Division

You will be provided with a calculator which you will be allowed to use for the entire duration of the numerical ability test. You will not be allowed to bring your own calculator.

TIPS FOR PASSING THE NUMERICAL REASONING TEST

- Try plenty of sample test questions in the build up to the assessment.
- You are permitted to use a calculator during the numerical reasoning test – one will be provided for you on the day at the assessment centre.
- Try to work quickly yet accurately through the test. If you miss a question then make sure you leave a gap on the answer sheet.
- If you generally struggle with this type of test then consider getting a personal tutor.
- During the test do not concentrate on the other candidates and how fast they are working. Keep your head down and focus only on your own performance.

I have now provided you with a number of sample numeracy tests to help you prepare.

NUMERICAL REASONING PRACTICE TESTS
PART ONE

Try to answer the questions quickly and without the use of a calculator.

You have 5 minutes in which to answer the 14 questions.

EXERCISE 1

1. A wallet has been found containing one £20 note, five £5 notes, a fifty pence coin and three 2 pence coins. How much is in the wallet?

Answer [   ]

2. Subtract 200 from 500, add 80, subtract 30 and multiply by 2. What number do you have?

Answer [   ]

3. A multi-storey car park has 8 floors and can hold 72 cars on each floor. In addition to this there is also allocation for 4 disabled parking spaces per floor. How many spaces are there in the entire car park?

Answer [   ]

4. A man saves £12.50 per month. How much would he have saved after 1 year?

   Answer [   ]

5. If there have been 60 accidents along one stretch of a motorway in the last year, how many on average have occurred each month?

   Answer [   ]

6. Out of 40,000 applicants only 4,000 are likely to be successful. What percentage will fail?

   Answer [   ]

7. What percentage of 400 is 100?

   Answer [   ]

8. Malcolm's shift commences at 0615 hours. If his shift is 10.5 hours long what time will he finish?

   Answer [   ]

9. If Mary can bake 12 cakes in 2 hours how many will she bake in 10 hours?

   Answer [   ]

10.   If there are 24 hours in the day. How many hours are there in one week?

Answer

11.   Susan has 10 coins and gives 5 of them to Steven and the remainder to Alan. Alan gives 3 of his coins to Steven who in turn gives half of his back to Susan. How many is Susan left with?

Answer

12.   Add 121 to 54. Now subtract 75 and multiply by 10. What is the result?

Answer

13.   Ahmed leaves for work at 8am and arrives at work at 9.17am. He then leaves work at 4.57pm and arrives back at home at 6.03pm. How many minutes has Ahmed spent travelling?

Answer

14.   A car travels at 30 km/h for the first hour, 65km/h for the second hour, 44 km/h for the third hour and 50 km/h for the fourth hour. What is the car's average speed over the 4-hour journey?

Answer

EXERCISE 2

You are not permitted to use a calculator during this exercise.

You have 10 minutes in which to answer 20 multiple-choice questions

1. Your friends tell you their electricity bill has gone up from £40 per month to £47 per month. How much extra are they now paying per year?

    A. £84 **B.** £85 **C.** £83 **D.** £86 **E.** £82

    Answer [   ]

2. A woman earns a salary of £32,000 per year. How much would she earn in 15 years?

    A. £280,000 **B.** £380,000 **C.** £480,000 **D.** £260,000 **E.** £460,000

    Answer [   ]

3. If a police officer walks the beat for 6 hours at a pace of 4km/h, how much ground will she have covered after the 6 hours is over?

    A. 20km **B.** 21km **C.** 22km **D.** 23km **E.** 24km

    Answer [   ]

4. It takes Malcolm 45 minutes to walk 6 miles to work. At what pace does he walk?

    A. 7 mph   **B.** 4 mph   **C.** 6 mph   **D.** 5 mph   **E.** 8 mph

    Answer

5. Ellie spends 3 hours on the phone talking to her friend abroad. If the call costs 12 pence per 5 minutes, how much does the call cost in total?

    A. £3.30   **B.** £4.32   **C.** £3.32   **D.** £4.44   **E.** £3.44

    Answer

6. A woman spends £27 in a retail store. She has a discount voucher that reduces the total cost to £21.60. How much discount does the voucher give her?

    A. 5%   **B.** 10%   **C.** 15%   **D.** 20%   **E.** 25%

    Answer

7. A group of 7 men spend £21.70 on a round of drinks. How much does each of them pay if the bill is split evenly?

    A. £3.00   **B.** £65.10   **C.** £3.10   **D.** £3.15   **E.** £3.20

    Answer

8.   45,600 people attend a football match to watch Manchester United play Tottenham Hotspur. If there are 32,705 Manchester United supporters at the game, how many Tottenham Hotspur supporters are there?

A. 12,985   **B.** 13,985   **C.** 12,895   **D.** 12,185   **E.** 14, 985

Answer [   ]

9.   The police are called to attend a motorway accident involving a coach full of passengers. A total of 54 people are on board, 17 of whom are injured. How many are not injured?

A. 40   **B.** 39   **C.** 38   **D.** 37   **E.** 36

Answer [   ]

10.   A car journey usually takes 6 hrs and 55 minutes, but on one occasion the car stops for a total of 47 minutes. How long does the journey take on this occasion?

A. 6 hrs 40 mins   **B.** 5 hrs 45 mins   **C.** 7 hrs 40 mins
D. 7 hrs 42 mins   **E.** 6 hrs 42 mins

Answer [   ]

11. There are 10 people in a team. Five of them weigh 70 kg each and the remaining 5 weigh 75 kg each. What is the average weight of the team?

A. 72.5 kg   **B.** 71.5 kg   **C.** 70.5 kg   **D.** 72 kg   **E.** 71 kg

Answer [   ]

12. A kitchen floor takes 80 tiles to cover. A man buys 10 boxes, each containing 6 tiles. How many more boxes does he need to complete the job?

A. 2 boxes   **B.** 4 boxes   **C.** 6 boxes   **D.** 8 boxes   **E.** 10 boxes

Answer [   ]

13. How much money does it cost to buy 12 packets of crisps at 47 pence each?

A. £6.45   **B.** £5.64   **C.** £6.54   **D.** £4.65   **E.** £5.46

Answer [   ]

14. A motorcyclist is travelling at 78 mph on a road where the speed limit is 50 mph. How much over the speed limit is he?

A. 20 mph   **B.** 22 mph   **C.** 26 mph   **D.** 28 mph   **E.** 30 mph

Answer

15. A removal firm loads 34 boxes onto a van. If there are 27 boxes still to be loaded, how many boxes are there in total?

A. 49   **B.** 50   **C.** 61   **D.** 52   **E.** 53

Answer

16. When paying a bill at the bank you give the cashier one £20 note, two £5 notes, four £1 coins, six 10p coins and two 2p coins. How much have you given him?

A. £34.64   **B.** £43.46   **C.** £34.46   **D.** £63.44   **E.** £36.46

Answer

17. If you pay £97.70 per month on your council tax bill, how much would you pay quarterly?

A. £293.30   **B.** £293.20   **C.** £293.10   **D.** £293.00   **E.** £292.90

Answer

18. Four people eat a meal at a restaurant. The total bill comes to £44.80. How much do they need to pay each?

A. £10.00 **B.** £10.10 **C.** £10.20 **D.** £11.10 **E.** £11.20

Answer

19. A worker is required to work for 8 hours a day. He is entitled to three 20-minute breaks and one 1-hour lunch break during that 8-hour period. If he works for 5 days per week, how many hours will he have worked after 4 weeks?

A. 12 hours **B.** 14 hours **C.** 120 hours **D.** 140 hours **E.** 150 hours

Answer

20. If there are 610 metres in a mile, how many metres are there in 4 miles?

A. 240 **B.** 2040 **C.** 2044 **D.** 2440 **E.** 244

Answer

ANSWERS TO NUMERICAL REASONING QUESTIONS

Exercise 1

1. £45.56

2. 700

3. 608

4. £150

5. 5

6. 90%

7. 25%

8. 1645 hours or 4.45pm

9. 60 cakes

10. 168

11. 4

12. 1000

13. 143 minutes

14. 47.25 km/h

Exercise 2

1. A. £84

In this question you need to first work out the difference in their electricity bill. Subtract £40 from £47 to be left with £7. Now you need to calculate how much extra they are paying per year. If there are 12 months in a year then you need to multiply £7 by 12 months to reach your answer of £84.

2. C. £480,000

The lady earns £32,000 per year. To work out how much she earns in 15 years, you must multiply £32,000 by 15 years to reach your answer of £480,000.

3. E. 24km

To work this answer out all you need to do is multiply the 6 hours by the 4 km/h to reach the total of 24 km. Remember that she is walking at a pace of 4 km per hour for a total of 6 hours.

4. E. 8mph

Malcolm walks 6 miles in 45 minutes, which means he is walking two miles every 15 minutes. Therefore, he would walk 8 miles in 60 minutes (1 hour), so he is walking at 8 mph.

5. B. £4.32

If the call costs 12 pence for every 5 minutes then all you need to do is calculate how many 5 minutes there are in the 3-hour telephone call. There are 60 minutes in every hour, so therefore there are 180 minutes in 3 hours. 180 minutes divided by 5 minutes will give you 36. To get your answer, just multiply 36 by 12 pence to reach your answer of £4.32

6. D. 20%

This type of question can be tricky, especially when you don't have a calculator! The best way to work out the answer is to first of all work out how much 10% discount would give you off the total price. If £27 is the total price, then 10% would be a £2.70 discount. In monetary terms the woman has received £5.40 in discount. If 10% is a £2.70 discount then 20% is a £5.40 discount.

7. C. £3.10

Divide £21.70 by 7 to reach your answer of £3.10.

8. C. 12,895

Subtract 32,705 from 45,600 to reach your answer of 12,895.

9. D. 37

Subtract 17 from 54 to reach your answer of 37.

10. D. 7 hrs 42 minutes

Add the 47 minutes to the normal journey time of 6 hrs and 55 minutes to reach your answer of 7 hrs and 42 minutes.

11. A. 72.5 kg

To calculate the average weight, you need to first of all add each weight together. Therefore, (5 x 70) + (5 x 75) = 725 kg. To find the average weight you must now divide the 725 by 10, which will give you the answer 72.5 kg.

12. B. 4 boxes

The man has 10 boxes, each of which contains 6 tiles. He therefore has a total of 60 tiles. He now needs a further 20 tiles to cover the total floor area. If there are 6 tiles in a box then he will need a further 4 boxes (24 tiles).

13. B. £5.64

Multiply 12 by 47 pence to reach your answer of £5.64.

14. D. 28 mph

Subtract 50 mph from 78 mph to reach your answer of 28 mph.

15. C. 61

Add 34 to 27 to reach your answer of 61 boxes.

16. A. £34.64

Add all of the currency together to reach the answer of £34.64.

17. C. £293.10

To reach the answer you must multiply £97.70 by 3. Remember, a quarter is every 3 months.

18. E. £11.20

Divide £44.80 by 4 people to reach your answer of £11.20.

19. C. 120 hours

First of all you need to determine how many 'real' hours he works each day. Subtract the total sum of breaks from 8 hours to reach 6 hours per day. If he works 5 days per week then he is working a total of 30 hours per week. Multiply 30 hours by 4 weeks to reach your answer of 120 hours.

20. D. 2440 metres

Multiply 4 by 610 metres to reach your answer of 2440 metres.

NUMERICAL REASONING PRACTICE TESTS
PART TWO

You will have 12 minutes to complete 25 questions.

You will be allowed to use a calculator during the numerical reasoning test.

PRACTICE TEST 1

1. A garage is selling three used cars. The mileage on the first is 139,500, the mileage on the second is 120,500, and the mileage on the third is 160,000. What is the average mileage of the three used cars?

   A. 140,000

   B. 145,000

   C. 150,000

   D. 135,000

   E. 130,000

2. You are called to an accident 120 miles away. It takes you 1 hour 30 minutes to arrive at the accident site. What speed have you been driving at?

    A. 80 mph

    B. 60 mph

    C. 40 mph

    D. 50 mph

    E. 45 mph

3. On a patrol around the local town you walk 10 miles. It takes you 2 hours. What speed do you walk at in miles per hour?

    A. 60 mph

    B. 20 mph

    C. 10 mph

    D. 5 mph

    E. 15 mph

4. During a traffic patrol you average 30 mph over 1 hour 20 minutes. What distance have you covered in this time?

    A. 32 miles

    B. 40 miles

    C. 50 miles

    D. 43 miles

    E. 45 miles

5. Sam, Steve and Mark are brothers. Sam is 36, Steve is 28 and Mark is
    26. What is their average age?

    A. 29

    B. 32

    C. 31

    D. 33

    E. 30

6. There are four suspects in a police line up. Suspect A is 1.20m tall,
    suspect B is 1.25m tall, suspect C is 1.55m tall and suspect D is 1.6m
    tall. What is the average height of the suspects?

    A. 1.41m

    B. 1.40m

    C. 1.42m

    D. 1.39m

    E. 1.37m

7. The perimeter of the police dog training yard is 240 metres. The yard
    has a square perimeter. What is the average length of a side of the
    yard?

    A. 40 metres

    B. 50 metres

    C. 60 metres

    D. 120 metres

    E. 130 metres

8. The police are escorting approximately 540 football fans to the train station. A train can carry 135 people. How many trains will be needed to transport the fans?

   A. 2 to 3

   B. 4 to 5

   C. 6 to 7

   D. 8 to 9

   E. 9 to 10

9. Darren commutes to and from work every day from Monday to Friday. His office is 40 miles away from his house. How many miles does Darren drive per week?

   A. 200

   B. 400

   C. 800

   D. 1,000

   E. 1,200

10. John runs a marathon (26 miles) with 69 other runners. Every single runner completes the marathon. What is the combined distance run by all the runners?

   A. 1784

   B. 1830

   C. 1794

   D. 1820

   E. 1824

11. You bicycle for 2 hours at an average speed of 18 mph. What distance have you travelled in total?

    A. 9 miles

    B. 20 miles

    C. 36 miles

    D. 24 miles

    E. 22 miles

12. John is a tree surgeon who is paid to cut down a dead oak tree. The tree is 90 metres tall. John has to cut the tree into 4.5m sections. How many cuts will he have to make?

    A. 10

    B. 45

    C. 30

    D. 40

    E. 20

13. You own a market stall and sell 216 apples. You have sold apples to 36 customers. On average how many apples did each customer buy?

    A. 4

    B. 6

    C. 8

    D. 12

    E. 14

14. The Metropolitan Police have 1,200 police officers on duty. They want 300 areas patrolled. How many police officers should go on each patrol?

    A. 2

    B. 3

    C. 5

    D. 6

    E. 4

15. A leisure complex has three pools: pool A, pool B and pool C. What is the area of swimming pool A?

    A. 6 m²

    B. 10 m²

    C. 12 m²

    D. 14 m²

    E. 21 m²

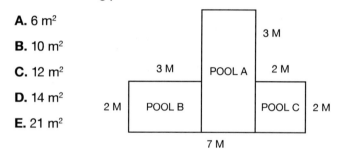

16. What is the average weekly wage of a team of five people whose individual wages are: £59.00, £61.00, £64.00, £76.00 and £80.00?

    A. £64

    B. £68

    C. £73

    D. £76

    E. £77

17. Response times to emergency calls vary throughout the week; on Monday it is 7 minutes, on Tuesday it's 7 minutes, on Wednesday it's 5 minutes, on Thursday it's 6 minutes, on Friday it's 9 minutes, on Saturday it's 8 minutes and finally on Sunday it's 7 minutes. What is the average response time?

    A. 6 minutes

    B. 5 minutes

    C. 8 minutes

    D. 9 minutes

    E. 7 minutes

18. There are 7 new PCSO's at a Wolverhampton police station. Their ages are 18, 19, 21, 24, 28, 29 and 36. What is their average age?

    A. 22 years old

    B. 24 years old

    C. 25 years old

    D. 26 years old

    E. 27 years old

19. There are 150 guests at a Spanish holiday complex. 50 of the guests are British, 35 are German, 10 are French, and 5 are Italian. The rest of the guests are Spanish. What percentage of guests are Spanish?

    A. 33.33%

    B. 32%

    C. 33%

    D. 66.66%

    E. 70%

20. Using the chart below, on average how many people would use the bus over a 4-month period?

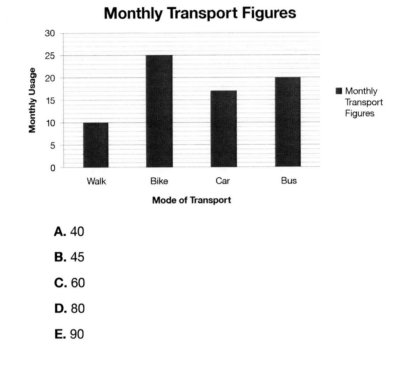

Monthly Transport Figures

A. 40

B. 45

C. 60

D. 80

E. 90

21. Using the chart above, calculate the combined total of people who walk and use a bike as a mode of transport per month?

A. 25

B. 30

C. 35

D. 40

E. 45

22. The police receive 1,200 applications for every 60 available posts. What is this as a fraction?

    A. 4/1

    B. 20/1

    C. 30/1

    D. 40/1

    E. 45/1

23. A container ship carries 1,000 barrels. Each barrel contains 330 litres of oil. How much oil is contained in the barrels?

    A. 330 litres

    B. 3,300 litres

    C. 33,000 litres

    D. 330,000 litres

    E. 3,300,000 litres

24. A bike company has 12 factories each producing 102 bikes a day. How many bikes does the company produce per day?

    A. 1,004

    B. 1,040

    C. 1,204

    D. 1,224

    E. 1,226

25. A carpet factory operates 24 hours a day. If the factory produces 10 carpets an hour, how many carpets are produced in a day?

    A. 220

    B. 240

    C. 260

    D. 280

    E. 290

PRACTICE TEST 2

1. In a biscuit tin there are 28 biscuits. If you were to divide these equally between a family of 4, how many biscuits would each family member get?

    A. 7

    B. 4

    C. 8

    D. 3.5

    E. 5

2. A plane can carry 180 passengers. There are 36 rows on the plane. How many passengers are there on each row?

    A. 9

    B. 6

    C. 7

    D. 8

    E. 5

3. You have been driving for 2 hours 15 minutes at a constant speed of 48 mph. How far have you driven so far?

    A. 180 miles

    B. 108 miles

    C. 104 miles

    D. 140 miles

    E. 144 miles

4.   A sprinter runs 200 metres in 22 seconds. How long would it take him to run 2,000 metres if he continued to run at the same speed?

   A. 3 minutes 40 seconds

   B. 3 minutes 20 seconds

   C. 4 minutes 20 seconds

   D. 3 minutes 15 seconds

   E. 4 minutes 15 seconds

5.   Samantha is a carpenter. She makes 3 oak tables for a family. The first table top measures 0.75 x 2 metres, the second measures 1.5 x 3 metres and the third measures 1.0 x 3 metres. What is the average area of the table tops?

   A. 5 m^2

   B. 4 m^2

   C. 3 m^2

   D. 2 m^2

   E. 2.5 m^2

6.   Five students buy a pizza each. Each pizza costs £5.20. The students are each given 10% discount. What is the total bill for the students?

   A. £23.20

   B. £23.40

   C. £23.60

   D. £24.40

   E. £24.60

7. At a campsite there are 240 tents. During a flood, 2.5% of the tents
    are damaged. How many tents were damaged during the flood?

   A. 6

   B. 8

   C. 5

   D. 9

   E. 4

8. In your savings account there is £13,000. You decide to withdraw 40%
    to buy a car. How much money do you withdraw?

   A. £520

   B. £5,200

   C. £7,200

   D. £8,000

   E. £8,200

9. You own a Ford Fiesta which is currently worth £8000. Since you
    bought the car it has depreciated in value by 30% of its original value.
    How much was the original value of the vehicle?

   A. £8,240

   B. £11,400

   C. £10,400

   D. £12,400

   E. £12,450

10. A ticket for a football match costs £12. If 12,000 people go to the game, how much in total will ticket sales make?

    A. £14,400

    B. £144,000

    C. £288,000

    D. £144,0000

    E. £420,000

11. A solicitor charges £28 per hour for legal services. If you hired a solicitor for 12 hours, how much would you be charged?

    A. £326

    B. £336

    C. £374

    D. £436

    E. £442

12. At Uxbridge Grammar there are 200 students. 15 of the students get straight A's. What is this as a percentage?

    A. 7.5%

    B. 10%

    C. 15%

    D. 30%

    E. 45%

13. You find a missing wallet in the street. It contains a £10 note, two £5 notes, three £1 coins, a 50p coin and six 2p coins. How much is in the wallet?

    A. £22.72

    B. £22.62

    C. £24.62

    D. £23.56

    E. £23.62

14. Your car does 35 miles to the gallon. The car takes 8 gallons of petrol full. If you were to drive 560 miles how much petrol would you need?

    A. 12 gallon

    B. 14 gallons

    C. 16 gallons

    D. 18 gallons

    E. 24 gallons

15. Two farmers, Jack and Tom, both own adjoining fields. What is the total combined area of both Jack's and Tom's fields?

    A. 160m²

    B. 240m²

    C. 800m²

    D. 1600m²

    E. 2400m²

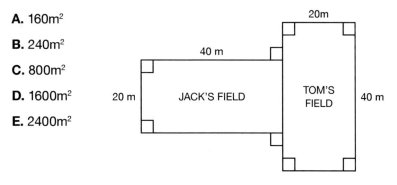

16. On average a bank repossesses 3 out of 150 homes every year. The village of Claxby has 1,000 homes. Under the above principle, how many homes would be repossessed in the village?

  A. 10

  B. 15

  C. 20

  D. 25

  E. 30

17. A school has 15 classes with 23 students in each class. How many students are at the school?

  A. 245

  B. 325

  C. 335

  D. 445

  E. 345

18. A restaurant serves 60 customers a night. If on average each customer spends £30, what is the total average for the night?

  A. £180

  B. £1,600

  C. £2,400

  D. £1,800

  E. £1,260

19. A chocolate bar costs 59p. If you were to buy 6 chocolate bars, how much would it cost you?

    A. £3.34

    B. £3.45

    C. £3.54

    D. £4.24

    E. £4.14

20. You fly a three-leg journey in a light aircraft. The total distance covered is 270 miles. What is the average distance of each leg?

    A. 70 miles

    B. 80 miles

    C. 90 miles

    D. 135 miles

    E. 140 miles

21. A team of 12 explorers find the wreck of a ship. The ship contains 6 gold bars each worth £120,000. How much money does each team member make?

    A. £40,000

    B. £60,000

    C. £100,000

    D. £120,000

    E. £130,000

22. Below is a pie-chart representing crime in the town of Upton. Based on an estimated 100 crimes, use the pie-chart below to estimate the number of burglary-related crimes.

Daily Crime Figures — Upton

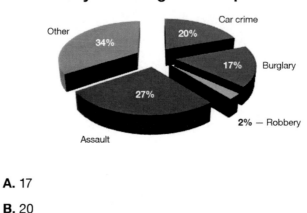

A. 17

B. 20

C. 27

D. 34

E. 170

23. A magazine on average contains 110 pages. If you bought seven magazines, how many pages are there in total?

    A. 700

    B. 720

    C. 740

    D. 770

    E. 780

24. A car is travelling at 72 miles per hour. How many miles will it have travelled in 45 minutes?

    A. 54

    B. 52

    C. 50

    D. 48

    E. 46

25. If carpet costs 1.20 per metre, how much will 35 metres of carpet cost?

    A. £45.00

    B. £43.75

    C. £44.00

    D. £46.75

    E. £42.00

PRACTICE TEST 3

1. If 70% of £500 has been spent, how much money remains?

    A. £125

    B. £130

    C. £140

    D. £150

    E. £160

2. A multi-storey office has 7 floors, and each floor has 49 employees. How many members of staff work in the multi-storey office?

    A. 257

    B. 343

    C. 357

    D. 423

    E. 475

3. Following some road works on the M1 the highways agency need their 5 vehicles to collect 1,250 cones. On average how many cones do each of the 5 vehicles have to collect?

    A. 125

    B. 200

    C. 250

    D. 500

    E. 525

4.   Laura buys three items: a pair of shoes, a dress, and a coat. The
     items totalled £340. If the shoes were £59.99 and the coat was
     £139.99, how much was the dress?

     A. £138.02

     B. £138.00

     C. £140.02

     D. £142.00

     E. £144.00

5.   At Telford school there are 200 school students. 25 students get
     straight A's. What is this as a percentage?

     A. 12.5%

     B. 10%

     C. 15%

     D. 30%

     E. 25%

6.   A carton of milk costs £1.19. How much change would you have left
     from £5.00 if you bought one carton?

     A. £2.81

     B. £3.61

     C. £3.71

     D. £3.81

     E. £4.05

7. You are driving down a motorway at 108 mph. How far do you travel in 25 minutes?

    A. 47 miles

    B. 45 miles

    C. 44 miles

    D. 42 miles

    E. 41 miles

8. A fast jet is flying at a speed of 270 mph. The distance from airfield A to airfield B is 90 miles. How long does it take to fly from A to B?

    A. 20 minutes

    B. 24 minutes

    C. 22 minutes

    D. 26 minutes

    E. 28 minutes

9. You are travelling down a motorway. Your journey has lasted 50 minutes and you have covered 125 miles. What speed have you been travelling at?

    A. 162 mph

    B. 155 mph

    C. 160 mph

    D. 152 mph

    E. 150 mph

10. The police on average respond to 25 emergency calls a day. How many do they respond to in a week?

    A. 160

    B. 165

    C. 170

    D. 175

    E. 180

11. Lincolnshire, Yorkshire and Lancashire all have new police helicopters. It takes the Lincolnshire helicopter 15 minutes to fly to Leeds, the Lancashire helicopter takes 35 minutes and the Yorkshire helicopter takes 10 minutes. What is the average time it takes these three helicopters to get to Leeds?

    A. 15 minutes

    B. 20 minutes

    C. 25 minutes

    D. 30 minutes

    E. 35 minutes

12. A car park has 500 available spaces. On a busy day 75% of these are full. How many full car parking spaces are there on a busy day?

    A. 375

    B. 350

    C. 325

    D. 320

    E. 310

13. You have £50 in your wallet and spend 70% of it on shopping. How much money have you spent on shopping?

    A. £30

    B. £35

    C. £40

    D. £50

    E. £45

14. The Metropolitan police force has 120,000 officers. 3% of these officers are due to retire. How many officers will retire?

    A. 360,000

    B. 36,000

    C. 360

    D. 36

    E. 3,600

15. The road tax for your car cost £120 in 2007. In 2008 it increases by 10%. How much is the road tax in 2008?

    A. £121.20

    B. £132

    C. £142

    D. £152

    E. £152.20

16. A school decides to buy 12 laptops costing £850 each. What is the combined cost for the 12 laptops?

    A. £10,200

    B. £10,400

    C. £10,500

    D. £10,600

    E. £10,800

17. A metre of wool costs 62p. How much would it cost to buy 6 metres of wool?

    A. £3.72

    B. £3.62

    C. £3.82

    D. £4.72

    E. £5.12

18. Sally is riding her horse in a cross country competition. She has been told that she has to complete the course in 2 hours and 30 minutes. If divided into equal quarters, how long should she aim to spend completing each phase?

    A. 35 minutes

    B. 37.5 minutes

    C. 35.5 minutes

    D. 38.5 minutes

    E. 39.5 minutes

19. There are 18 teams entered in a rugby competition. If there are 6 changing rooms, how many teams use each changing room?

    A. 2

    B. 4

    C. 6

    D. 3

    E. 5

20. Using the diagram below, calculate the perimeter of the inner rectangle?

    A. 16.4 cm

    B. 17.2 cm

    C. 17.8 cm

    D. 18.4 cm

    E. 18.8 cm

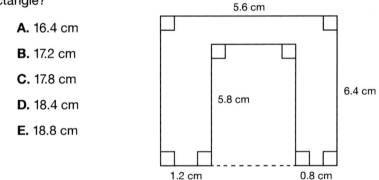

21. A room measures 20m by 5m. If I wanted to carpet 50% of it and I had 60 square metres of carpet available, how many square metres would I have left after finishing the task?

    A. 5m²

    B. 10m²

    C. 15m²

    D. 20m²

    E. 25m²

22. If a ferry journey of 490 miles takes 7 hours, what is the average speed of the ferry?

   A. 55 mph

   B. 60 mph

   C. 65 mph

   D. 70 mph

   E. 80 mph

23. A multi-storey car park has 8 levels. Each level has 111 car parking spaces. How many cars will be in the car park when it is full?

   A. 784

   B. 888

   C. 988

   D. 8,888

   E. 9,988

24. The office sweepstake wins £1,500. If this is divided by 25 employees, how much does each employee win?

   A. £30

   B. £40

   C. £60

   D. £80

   E. £85

25. Below is a line graph showing car sales for Manby Autos from January to April. Calculate the total combined car sales for February and March.

A. 900

B. 8,000

C. 9,000

D. 10,000

E. 12,000

PRACTICE TEST 4

1. A yearly golf subscription costs £150 in 2007. It is expected to rise by 15% in 2008. How much will the yearly subscription cost in 2008?

    A. £172.50

    B. £172.20

    C. £172

    D. £165.72

    E. £162.50

2. In a cross country competition there are 138 runners, 23 runners do not finish the race. What is this as a fraction?

    A. 1/5

    B. 1/6

    C. 1/8

    D. 1/12

    E. 1/4

3. A football pitch is approximately 110 metres long. If you had 11 football pitches, one after the other, how long would the total distance be?

    A. 1,110 metres

    B. 1,420 metres

    C. 1,390 metres

    D. 1,440 metres

    E. 1,210 metres

4. One out of twelve people in a group of football fans support Manchester United. If there are 2880 football fans, how many do not support Manchester United?

    A. 2420

    B. 2640

    C. 2680

    D. 2740

    E. 2520

5. A constable leaves the house at 08.00 hours and returns at 14.45 hours. How many hours has he been away from home?

    A. 5 hours 50 minutes

    B. 5 hours 45 minutes

    C. 6 hours 50 minutes

    D. 6 hours 45 minutes

    E. 6 hours 15 minutes

6. You go to your local supermarket. You decide to buy some tomato soup. Each tin costs 14p. How much will 6 tins cost in total?

    A. 60p

    B. 64p

    C. 70p

    D. 84p

    E. 86p

7. One carpet tile measures 50cm by 50cm. How many tiles are required to cover a floor which measures 10m by 2m?

   A. 70

   B. 75

   C. 80

   D. 85

   E. 90

8. One power station supplies power to 34,000 homes. How many homes would 4 power stations supply?

   A. 126,000

   B. 128,000

   C. 138,000

   D. 148,000

   E. 136,000

9. A drum contains 23 litres of oil. If a ship carries 11 drums of oil onboard, how many litres of oil are there altogether?

   A. 233 litres

   B. 241 litres

   C. 253 litres

   D. 263 litres

   E. 266 litres

10. A football match has an average of 32,000 spectators. There are 26 football matches a year. What is the total number of spectators throughout the year?

    A. 83,200

    B. 832,000

    C. 964,000

    D. 110,600

    E. 124,000

11. A library has 25 shelves of books. Each shelf holds 700 books. How many books are in the library?

    A. 1,750

    B. 17,050

    C. 17,500

    D. 35,000

    E. 38,500

12. At an allotment there are 3 plots: plot A, plot B and plot C. Using the diagram below, calculate the area of plot B.

    A. 1,000 m²

    B. 2,500 m²

    C. 2,000 m²

    D. 3,000 m²

    E. 100 m²

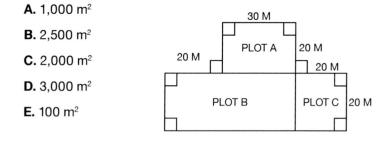

13. What is the average value of the following: 14, 28, 47, 47, 60 and 104?

    A. 50

    B. 53

    C. 55

    D. 60

    E. 62

14. There are 44 police forces in the United Kingdom. Each police force has 14 Senior Officers. How many Senior Officers are there in total?

    A. 561

    B. 606

    C. 616

    D. 861

    E. 882

15. A company has to dismiss 1 out of 6 of their employees. If the company employs 636 people, how many will the company have to dismiss?

    A. 96

    B. 103

    C. 106

    D. 126

    E. 132

16. If 6 out of 24 police officers become traffic officers, what is this as a fraction?

      A. 1/4

      B. 2/4

      C. 1/8

      D. 1/6

      E. 1/3

17. You go to the local shop and buy a magazine costing £2.40 and a drink costing £1.12. How much change do you get from a £10 note?

      A. £6.52

      B. £4.48

      C. £5.52

      D. £6.48

      E. £6.56

18. A cruise ship can carry 90,000 passengers. On this occasion the ship is only 75% full. How many passengers are on board?

      A. 6,750

      B. 13,500

      C. 54,500

      D. 67,500

      E. 68,250

19. A car garage sells 50 cars per month. 2 % of these are returned with engine problems. How many cars with engine problems are returned to the car garage each year?

    A. 6

    B. 9

    C. 13

    D. 15

    E. 12

20. A Formula 1 car drives 660 miles in 3 hours 40 minutes. What is its average speed?

    A. 160 mph

    B. 190 mph

    C. 180 mph

    D. 185 mph

    E. 190 mph

21. You can run 2 miles in 18 minutes. How long does it take you to run 0.5 miles at this speed?

    A. 4 minutes 30 seconds

    B. 5 minutes

    C. 6 minute 30 seconds

    D. 4 minutes 20 seconds

    E. 5 minutes 10 seconds

22. You walk to school and it takes you 20 minutes. You know that you walk an average of 3 mph. How far is school from your house?

    A. 2 miles

    B. 1 mile

    C. 6 miles

    D. 4 miles

    E. 5 miles

23. A farmer has 650 sheep. He keeps his sheep in 5 large fields. How many sheep does he have in each field?

    A. 120

    B. 130

    C. 150

    D. 160

    E. 170

24. A delivery driver has to drive on average 12,000 miles a month. If the driver works every day in April, how many miles does he have to drive each day?

    A. 200 miles

    B. 300 miles

    C. 350 miles

    D. 387 miles

    E. 400 miles

25. You withdraw 30% of your savings from an account which holds £600. How much remains in the account?

    A. £360

    B. £390

    C. £420

    D. £430

    E. £450

PRACTICE TEST 5

1. A cruise ship has 13 rows of windows. If each row has 39 windows, how many windows are there in total?

    A. 498

    B. 507

    C. 527

    D. 618

    E. 627

2. In a car park there are 325 cars, and each car has 4 tyres and 1 spare tyre. How many tyres are there throughout the car park?

    A. 1,525

    B. 1,575

    C. 1,650

    D. 1,675

    E. 1,625

3. A greengrocer has a box of 360 strawberries. The greengrocer wants to make up punnets of strawberries, each with 36 strawberries in it. How many punnets of strawberries can the greengrocer make?

    A. 6

    B. 10

    C. 12

    D. 26

    E. 36

4. A ball of wool measures 3.3 metres. If you have 100 balls of wool, how many metres will there be?

    A. 3.30 metres

    B. 33.0 metres

    C. 330 metres

    D. 3,300 metres

    E. 660 metres

5. How many pieces of string measuring 1.25 metres in length can be cut from a ball which is 100m long?

    A. 12.5

    B. 125

    C. 80

    D. 250

    E. 250

6. One case containing 42 cartons of orange juice costs £6.30. How much will two cartons of orange juice cost?

    A. 10p

    B. 15p

    C. 25p

    D. 30p

    E. 45p

7. A moped is travelling at a speed of 35 mph. How long does it take to travel 7 miles?

    A. 6 minutes

    B. 10 minutes

    C. 24 minutes

    D. 8 minutes

    E. 12 minutes

8. A train travels a total distance of 540 miles at a constant speed of 90 mph. How long does the journey last?

    A. 360 minutes

    B. 320 minutes

    C. 240 minutes

    D. 300 minutes

9. What speed do you need to travel to go 100 miles in 2 hours?

    A. 25 mph

    B. 200 mph

    C. 10 mph

    D. 20 mph

    E. 50 mph

10. A prisoner has escaped from prison. The prison is 20 miles away. You need to get there in 15 minutes. How fast do you need to drive?

    A. 40 mph

    B. 60 mph

    C. 80 mph

    D. 85 mph

    E. 90 mph

11. A CD album has 49 minutes worth of songs. If each song is 3 minutes 30 seconds long, how many songs are on the album?

    A. 7

    B. 14

    C. 15

    D. 28

    E. 18

12. A coach driver is making a journey form Land's End to John O'Groats. This is a distance of 420 miles. He has to make 7 equal stops. How many miles apart does each stop have to be?

    A. 60

    B. 80

    C. 45

    D. 70

    E. 50

13. A train has 6 trams and each tram holds 80 tonnes of freight. What is the total weight of freight carried by the train?

    A. 380 tonnes

    B. 420 tonnes

    C. 480 tonnes

    D. 570 tonnes

    E. 580 tonnes

14. An office has 333 computer desks. If only 2/3 are used, how many are un-used?

    A. 33

    B. 90

    C. 111

    D. 222

    E. 22

15. Mike cycles every day for 30 minutes. How much time does he spend cycling over 8 days?

    A. 3.5 hours

    B. 4 hours

    C. 4.5 hours

    D. 5 hours

    E. 5.5 hours

16. A rugby club raises its annual subscription of £300 by 25%. What will the new subscription be?

    A. £345

    B. £360

    C. £370

    D. £375

    E. £385

17. A cinema ticket costs £5.00. If a pensioner is given a 15% discount, how much change will they get from a £20 note?

    A. £15.25

    B. £15.45

    C. £15.75

    D. £16.25

    E. £16.30

18. A circle has a diameter of 240 mm. What is the length, in centimetres, of the radius?

    A. 12 cm

    B. 18 cm

    C. 22 cm

    D. 6 cm

    E. 24 cm

19. Below is a bar chart showing yearly vegetable sales for a market in Castleton. What is the average yearly sale of mushrooms over the three years?

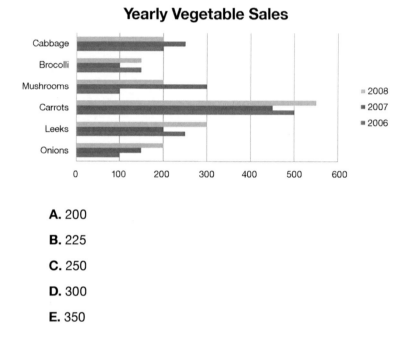

Yearly Vegetable Sales

    A. 200

    B. 225

    C. 250

    D. 300

    E. 350

20. Roger needs to lay new turf in his garden. The whole of the garden will need new turf. Calculate the area of the garden that will need new turf.

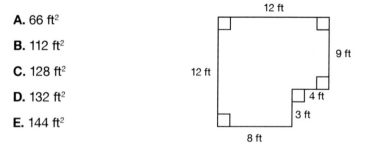

    A. 66 ft²

    B. 112 ft²

    C. 128 ft²

    D. 132 ft²

    E. 144 ft²

21. If I have £40 in my wallet and spend £13.75 of it, how much will I have left?

    A. £25.75

    B. £26.25

    C. £27.50

    D. £28.15

    E. £29.60

22. A motorist is travelling at 80mph. How far will he have travelled in 15 minutes?

    A. 10 miles

    B. 15 miles

    C. 12 miles

    D. 25 miles

    E. 20 miles

23. A prison cell holds two people. There are two prison areas: high risk and low risk. The high risk area has 123 cells and the low risk area has 334 cells. How many prisoners are there in the prison?

    A. 897

    B. 910

    C. 914

    D. 1,010

    E. 1,028

24. A food processing company has 10 people a week absent due to illness. How many people are absent due to illness in a year?

    A. 520

    B. 730

    C. 1,040

    D. 3,640

    E. 3,650

25. Balmoray Police operates a three-shift working pattern in each day. Each shift has to have 22 police officers on duty. How many officers are required for a days work?

    A. 66

    B. 62

    C. 60

    D. 86

    E. 132

PRACTICE TEST 6

1.   In the Johnson family there are 7 people; 3 of them are female. What is this as a fraction?

   A. 2/3

   B. 4/6

   C. 3/7

   D. 6/15

   E. 1/3

2.   You are at a traffic collision where a vehicle has crashed into a play area. As part of your documentation you need to calculate the area of the playing field. Using the diagram below, work out the area of the playing field and select the appropriate answer.

   A. 700 m²

   B. 900 m²

   C. 1,200 m²

   D. 1,300 m²

   E. 1,400 m²

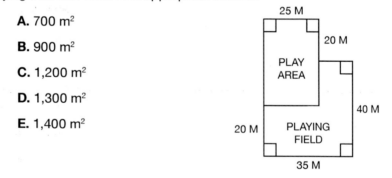

3.   Your yearly salary is £40,000. You also receive a yearly bonus which is 15% of your salary. How much do you earn per year?

   A. £40,060

   B. £40,600

   C. £46,000

   D. £49,000

   E. £56,000

4. On a housing estate there are 34,000 homes. Of these homes 63% are semi-detached, 30% are detached, and the remainder are terraced houses. How many houses are terraced?

    A. 23.8

    B. 238

    C. 2,380

    D. 2,680

    E. 23,800

5. You have two foot patrols a day. The total distance walked is 20 miles. If you walked an average speed of 4 mph, how long is each patrol?

    A. 5 hours

    B. 3 hours 30 minutes

    C. 4 hours

    D. 2 hours 30 minutes

    E. 4 hours 20 minutes

6. You are tasked to drive your boss to a meeting 100 miles away. You will be driving at 60 mph. If you set off at 10:20pm, what time would you arrive?

    A. 11:40pm

    B. 12:00pm

    C. 12:40pm

    D. 12:20pm

    E. 12:30pm

7. A criminal sprints at a speed of 10 metres every 2 seconds (10m/2 seconds). How long does it take him to run 1,000 metres if he continues at the same speed?

   A. 100 seconds

   B. 10 seconds

   C. 200 seconds

   D. 20 seconds

   E. 25 seconds

8. You are at a fruit and vegetable stall at a market. If one apple costs 41p, how much would it cost to buy 11 apples?

   A. £4.41

   B. £4.21

   C. £4.61

   D. £4.67

   E. £4.51

9. A car garage orders four new sport cars costing £41,000 each. How much in total has the garage spent on the new sports cars?

   A. £124,000

   B. £154,000

   C. £164,000

   D. £166,000

   E. £168,000

10. A water tank has a maximum capacity of 200 litres. If the tank is 80% full how many more litres are required to fill it to its maximum?

    A. 25 litres

    B. 40 litres

    C. 50 litres

    D. 55 litres

    E. 60 litres

11. If I spend £1.60, £2.35, £3.55 and £4.75 on a selection of goods, how much will I have spent in total?

    A. £10.65

    B. £11.60

    C. £11.55

    D. £12.25

    E. £12.55

12. Below is a chart showing snowfall across the Lincolnshire region in 2004 in centimetres. What is the combined snowfall for January and May?

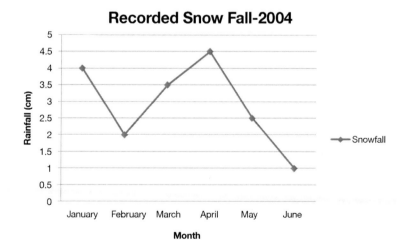

Recorded Snow Fall-2004

A. 5.5 cm

B. 6.0 cm

C. 6.5 cm

D. 7.0 cm

E. 8.5 cm

13. On Monday it takes Lucy 52 minutes to get to work. On Tuesday it takes 40 minutes, Wednesday takes 51 minutes, on Thursday it takes 1 hour 2 minutes and on Friday it takes 1 hour 30 minutes. How long did her average commute take?

    A. 58 minutes

    B. 62 minutes

    C. 60 minutes

    D. 61 minutes

    E. 59 minutes

14. Paul is a 100 metre sprinter. During a weekend-long competition he runs the distance in 11 seconds, 9 seconds, 9.5 seconds and 11.5 seconds. What is the average time that Paul runs 100 metres in?

    A. 9 seconds

    B. 10 seconds

    C. 11 seconds

    D. 10.25 seconds

    E. 10.5 seconds

15. One in fourteen people become a victim of car crime each year. In Saxby there are 224 people. On that basis, how many people per year experience car crime in Saxby?

    A. 14

    B. 16

    C. 18

    D. 20

    E. 22

16. Lisa's weekly newspaper bill is £5.50 and the delivery charge is 35p per week. How much does she have to pay over six weeks?

    A. £28.10

    B. £31.10

    C. £35.10

    D. £35.20

    E. £36.10

17. A gardener wants to gravel over the area shown below. One bag of gravel will cover 20 m². How many bags are needed to cover the entire garden?

    A. 40

    B. 55

    C. 65

    D. 75

    E. 130

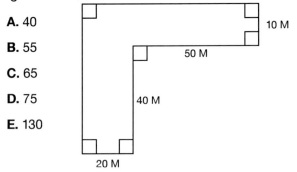

10 M

50 M

40 M

20 M

18. The gardener decides he is only going to gravel 20% of the garden. Using the above diagram, how many square metres will he be gravelling?

   A. 26 m²

   B. 300 m²

   C. 130 m²

   D. 240 m²

   E. 260 m²

19. You stop and search 40 people, and 8 of them are arrested for possession of a class A drug. What is this as a fraction?

   A. 1/3

   B. 1/4

   C. 1/6

   D. 1/10

   E. 1/5

20. There are 144 people entered into a raffle, 12 people each win a prize. What is this as a fraction?

   A. 1/6

   B. 1/8

   C. 1/12

   D. 1/24

   E. 1/10

21. At a music festival there are 35,000 festival goers, 5% of these are under 16 years of age. How many festival goers were under 16?

    A. 1500

    B. 1750

    C. 2500

    D. 3500

    E. 7000

22. At Christmas you buy 30 presents; 12 are bought for your family and 18 for your friends. What percentage was bought for your friends?

    A. 20%

    B. 30%

    C. 40%

    D. 60%

    E. 75%

23. Over one year, PC Smith files details of 600 drink driving cases. These are divided into 5 piles dependant upon how over the limit the drink driver was. If the piles are all equal sizes, how many are in each pile?

    A. 115 files

    B. 120 files

    C. 125 files

    D. 130 files

    E. 135 files

24. On average, 1 out of every 30 people experience back problems in their lifetime. Out of 900 people, how many will experience back problems?

    A. 20

    B. 30

    C. 60

    D. 90

    E. 120

25. Below are a toy company's monthly sale figures. Calculate the average toy sales per month for the year.

    A. 350

    B. 375

    C. 450

    D. 500

    E. 700

PRACTICE TEST 7

1. Billy can run 1.5 miles in 12 minutes. How long does it take him to run 12 miles if he continues at the same speed?

    A. 1 hour 26 minutes

    B. 1 hour 12 minutes

    C. 1 hour 36 minutes

    D. 1 hour 6 minutes

    E. 1 hour 20 minutes

2. Jennifer runs 39 miles in 4 hours 20 minutes. What was her average speed?

    A. 12 mph

    B. 10 mph

    C. 9 mph

    D. 7 mph

    E. 8 mph

3. A helicopter flies a distance of 840 miles in 6 hours. What speed is it flying at in miles per hour?

    A. 140 mph

    B. 160 mph

    C. 150 mph

    D. 145 mph

    E. 135 mph

4. Emma works 5 days a week. Everyday she drives 20 miles to work, and 20 miles back. She drives at an average speed of 30 mph. How much time does Emma spend driving to work and back each working week?

    A. 6 hours 40 minutes

    B. 6 hours 15 minutes

    C. 6 hours 20 minutes

    D. 6 hours 45 minutes

    E. 7 hours

5. You are driving to an incident at 96 mph. The incident is 24 miles away. How long will it take you to get to the incident?

    A. 12 minutes

    B. 15 minutes

    C. 10 minutes

    D. 20 minutes

    E. 25 minutes

6. You are driving at 42 mph for 20 minutes. How far have you come?

    A. 14 miles

    B. 20 miles

    C. 17 miles

    D. 15 miles

    E. 16 miles

7.   In a year 20,600 people are arrested. One quarter of these are over 50 years of age. How many people over 50 years of age are arrested?

   A. 4,150

   B. 4,300

   C. 5,350

   D. 5,200

   E. 5,150

8.   If 2 out of 10 entrants won at a dog show, how many would win if there were 100 entrants at the show?

   A. 10

   B. 15

   C. 20

   D. 35

   E. 40

9.   The pie chart below shows the percentage of aircraft sales across the world. If 10,000 aircraft were sold in total, how many were sold in the UK?

   A. 15,000

   B. 1,750

   C. 150

   D. 1,000

   E. 1,500

Aircraft Sales

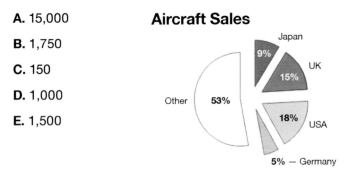

10. Using the pie chart above calculate, the combined aircraft sales for both the USA and other countries.

    A. 710

    B. 1,710

    C. 1,900

    D. 6,500

    E. 7,100

11. Calculate the perimeter of the shape below.

    A. 18.4 cm

    B. 28.0 cm

    C. 28.4 cm

    D. 32.0 cm

    E. 32.8 cm

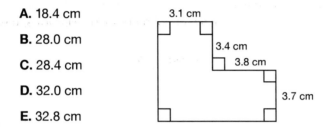

12. An office block has a length of 28 metres and width of 10 metres. What is the size of the floor space?

    A. 176 m²

    B. 240 m²

    C. 280 m²

    D. 440 m²

    E. 560 m²

13. An office has a floor space of 21,000 m². If 700 people work in the office, how much m² space does each employee have?

> **A.** 3 m²
>
> **B.** 30 m²
>
> **C.** 60 m²
>
> **D.** 90 m²
>
> **E.** 300 m²

14. New police boots cost £112; you are subsidised £42 from the force to contribute towards the boots. How much will you need to contribute?

> **A.** £60
>
> **B.** £62
>
> **C.** £58
>
> **D.** £74
>
> **E.** £70

15. I have £13 in my wallet and spend £4.37 shopping. How much do I have left?

> **A.** £8.73
>
> **B.** £7.63
>
> **C.** £8.63
>
> **D.** £6.85
>
> **E.** £6.53

16. How much do 24 boxes of chocolates cost at £4.10 each?

> A. £98.20
>
> B. £78.20
>
> C. £88.40
>
> D. £94.40
>
> E. £98.40

17. Police in Horncastle pull over 200 suspected drink drivers over a 6 month period. There are 36 people over the drink driving limit. Out of the 200, what percentage are over the legal limit?

> A. 16%
>
> B. 18%
>
> C. 24%
>
> D. 30%
>
> E. 36%

18. Each year 15,000 police officers are recruited in Scotland. 30% are female officers. How many male police officers are recruited in Scotland each year?

> A. 4500
>
> B. 7500
>
> C. 10500
>
> D. 12500
>
> E. 15000

19. What is the average age of a group of children whose individual ages are 11 years, 13 years, 9 years, 9 years, and 8 years?

     A. 10 years

     B. 11 years

     C. 12 years

     D. 13 years

     E. 14 years

20. How much would it cost to buy 26 jars of jam at £1.15 per jar?

     A. £26.90

     B. £27.60

     C. £28.50

     D. £29.45

     E. £29.90

21. There are 635 boxes in a lorry. How many boxes would there be in 3 lorries?

     A. 1,605

     B. 1,805

     C. 1,850

     D. 1,905

     E. 1,980

22. In a pick and mix you get 25 sweets in a bag for £4.00. How much does each sweet cost?

    A. £0.10

    B. £0.16

    C. £1.00

    D. £1.60

    E. £1.80

23. You are trying to decide where to go on a skiing holiday. To fly to Tignes in France will take 3 hours 30 minutes; to fly to Whistler in Canada will take 6 hours 50 minutes; and to fly to Switzerland will take 4 hours 40 minutes. What is the average journey time for all three different routes?

    A. 4 hours

    B. 5 hours

    C. 6 hours

    D. 7 hours

    E. 10 hours

24. PC Wood is carrying out research into the market value of narcotics. He is given four values for an eighth of an ounce of cannabis: £19, £22, £21.75, and £25.25. What is the average value for an eighth of an ounce of cannabis?

    A. £17

    B. £19

    C. £21

    D. £22

    E. £24

25. Your business has yearly profits of £520,000. There are 13 equal share holders in the company. How much does each individual make in profit?

        A. £20,000

        B. £30,000

        C. £35,000

        D. £40,000

        E. £42,000

PRACTICE TEST 8

1. At a football tournament there are 15 teams. Each team has a squad
    of twenty players. How many players are there in total?

    A. 200

    B. 300

    C. 400

    D. 450

    E. 500

2. The total number of hours worked by employees in a week is 390. If
    there are 13 employees, how many hours per work does each person
    work?

    A. 3 hours

    B. 20 hours

    C. 30 hours

    D. 45 hours

    E. 60 hours

3. The diagram below shows a playing field and a sand pit. Calculate the
    area of the playing field using the information displayed.

    A. 950 m²

    B. 1,400 m²

    C. 1,950 m²

    D. 2,400 m²

    E. 2,850 m²

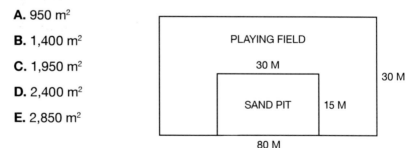

4.　Hampshire Police operate a three-shift working pattern each day. Each shift has to have 24 police officers on duty. How many officers are required for a week's work, Monday to Friday?

    A. 36

    B. 480

    C. 420

    D. 504

    E. 360

5.　Below is a scatter graph portraying sample height and shoe size for Class 4 at Edgbaston Primary School. What is the combined average shoe size for someone who is 160 cm tall and someone who is 180 cm tall?

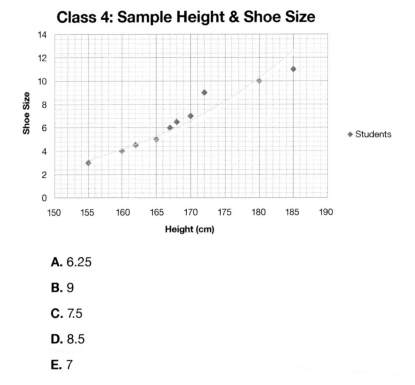

Class 4: Sample Height & Shoe Size

    A. 6.25

    B. 9

    C. 7.5

    D. 8.5

    E. 7

6. Using the scatter graph (and trend line) above, calculate the approximate shoe size of a student who is 175 cm in height.

>   **A.** 7
>
>   **B.** 7.5
>
>   **C.** 8
>
>   **D.** 8.5
>
>   **E.** 9

7. You need to measure the perimeter of a square house. You know that one side of the house measures 15.5 metres. What is the perimeter of the house?

>   **A.** 52 metres
>
>   **B.** 62 metres
>
>   **C.** 63 metres
>
>   **D.** 64 metres
>
>   **E.** 66 metres

8. A police officer has to put some marker cones out along a stretch of road. The road is 240 metres long and cones have to be placed 1.5 metres apart. How many cones will the police officer need?

>   **A.** 150
>
>   **B.** 160
>
>   **C.** 165
>
>   **D.** 170
>
>   **E.** 180

9. The school run in Milton Keynes takes 3 minutes if you drive at a speed of 30 mph. How far away is the school?

   A. 1″ miles

   B. 2 miles

   C. 3 miles

   D. 5″ miles

   E. 10 miles

10. You are flying at 240 mph. How far have you travelled in 12 minutes?

    A. 24 miles

    B. 48 miles

    C. 36 miles

    D. 20 miles

    E. 40 miles

11. You have arrived at an RTA (Road Traffic Accident) and immediately call for an ambulance. The ambulance is 12 miles from your current location. You have told the ambulance that you need it here in 5 minutes. What speed must the ambulance drive at to get to the RTA on time?

    A. 60 mph

    B. 140 mph

    C. 50 mph

    D. 144 mph

    E. 132 mph

12. There are 18 strawberries in a punnet. In a shop there are 12 punnets. How many strawberries are there in total?

    A. 132

    B. 162

    C. 316

    D. 432

    E. 216

13. You find a purse in the street. It contains a £10 note, a £5 note, four £2 coins, three £1 coins, a 50p coin, four 2p coins and a penny. How much is there in the purse?

    A. £22.59

    B. £22.49

    C. £24.69

    D. £25.69

    E. £26.59

14. A car park in Warrington issues 15 parking fines a week, each costing £60. How much does the car park make from fines every 4 weeks?

    A. £1,800

    B. £2,600

    C. £3,600

    D. £3,800

    E. £4,800

15. Mary goes food shopping 3 times a week. How many times does she go food shopping in a year?

    A. 156

    B. 158

    C. 166

    D. 226

    E. 256

16. The plan below shows a layout of your garden and vegetable plot. You want to lay decking over half of the garden. What area will the decking cover?

    A. 20 m²

    B. 100 m²

    C. 125 m²

    D. 175 m²

    E. 200 m²

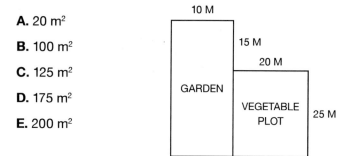

17. 15% of the vegetable plot is used to grow carrots. Using the above diagram calculate what area of the vegetable plot is used to grow carrots?

    A. 25 m²

    B. 37.5 m²

    C. 48 m²

    D. 50 m²

    E. 75 m²

18. At Lowbridge High School there are 180 students taking exams. 60 of these students gain A to C grades. What is this as a fraction?

    A. 1/4

    B. 1/3

    C. 2/3

    D. 1/6

    E. 1/5

19. Your family own 5 cars. 3 of the cars are red. What is this as a percentage?

    A. 30%

    B. 40%

    C. 60%

    D. 65%

    E. 70%

20. Whilst shopping I spend £1.60, £2.35, £5.60 and 74p. How much have I spent in total?

    A. £10.39

    B. £10.29

    C. £10.49

    D. £10.59

    E. £11.29

21. A car ownership survey discovered that out of 10,000 cars, 2,500 were Fords. What is this as a percentage?

    A. 20%

    B. 25%

    C. 30%

    D. 35%

    E. 40%

22. A motorbike is speeding at 180 mph. How far does it travel in 10 minutes?

    A. 60 miles

    B. 40 miles

    C. 30 miles

    D. 25 miles

    E. 20 miles

23. A train is travelling at a speed of 80 mph. The distance between station A and station B is 200 miles. How long will it take to get from station A to station B?

    A. 2 hours 15 minutes

    B. 2 hours 20 minutes

    C. 2 hours 35 minutes

    D. 2 hours 40 minutes

    E. 2 hours 30 minutes

24. You are running late for work and you have 30 minutes to get there on time. Your work is 25 miles away. What speed do you have to drive at so as not to be late?

      A. 75 mph

      B. 45 mph

      C. 50 mph

      D. 30 mph

      E. 15 mph

25. What speed would you need travel at to achieve 180 miles in 20 minutes?

      A. 360 mph

      B. 540 mph

      C. 270 mph

      D. 90 mph

      E. 100 mph

PRACTICE TEST 9

1. As a traffic officer you cover 360 miles a day. Over an 8-hour shift, what is your average speed for the day?

    A. 50 mph

    B. 60 mph

    C. 48 mph

    D. 45 mph

    E. 46 mph

2. A journey takes 2 hours and 30 minutes. You have been travelling at a speed of 70 mph. How far have you travelled?

    A. 160 miles

    B. 170 miles

    C. 175 miles

    D. 185 miles

    E. 190 miles

3. A garage is selling three used cars. The mileage on the first is 119,500; the mileage on the second is 140,500; the mileage on the third in 160,000. What is the average mileage of the three used cars?

    A. 140,000

    B. 142,000

    C. 145,000

    D. 150,000

    E. 135,000

4. At a restaurant you and your friend buy a king prawn salad (£6.95), some salmon fish cakes (£5.95), steak and chips (£11.50), chicken and chips (£10.25) and a chocolate cake (£3.95). You agree to split the bill equally. How much do you both pay?

    A. £19.50

    B. £19.40

    C. £19.30

    D. £19.20

    E. £19.10

5. In a restaurant you and your friend buy a salad (£3.95), scallops (£6.95), steak and chips (£12.60), chicken and chips (£9.15) and ice cream (£1.95). You agree to split the bill equally, how much do you both pay?

    A. £17.35

    B. £18.40

    C. £17.60

    D. £15.30

    E. £17.30

6. A company adds up the total number of sick days had by its employees. Out of the 52 weeks in a year it is calculated that, in total, employees have 13 weeks off sick. What is this as a percentage?

    A. 25%

    B. 20%

    C. 15%

    D. 10%

    E. 5%

7. Using the diagram below, calculate the perimeter of the lily bed.

   A. 70 m

   B. 75 m

   C. 90 m

   D. 95 m

   E. 100 m

8. A bag contains 5 litres of compost soil. You calculate that 5 litres of compost will cover an area of 2.5 m². Using the above diagram calculate how many bags of soil you will need to fill the tulip bed.

   A. 20 bags

   B. 100 bags

   C. 200 bags

   D. 250 bags

   E. 400 bags

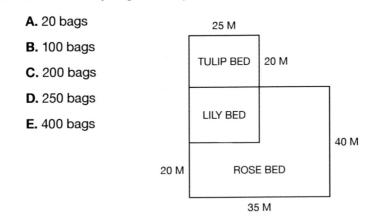

9. If the police air support unit flies at a speed of 120 mph for 12 minutes, how far has it travelled?

   A. 48 miles

   B. 26 miles

   C. 12 miles

   D. 24 miles

   E. 6 miles

10. A bus drives for 4 hours covering a total distance of 240 miles. What was his average speed in miles per hour?

    A. 120 mph

    B. 30 mph

    C. 40 mph

    D. 60 mph

    E. 50 mph

11. Five out of one hundred police officers are injured during duty every year. What is this as a fraction?

    A. 1/5

    B. 1/20

    C. 1/30

    D. 2/50

    E. 1/4

12. School dinners cost £4.75 each, and 200 children have dinners each day. How much is made from school dinners per day?

    A. £550

    B. £750

    C. £850

    D. £950

    E. £1,050

13. You have a meeting at 0900hrs. You leave your house at 0840hrs. The meeting location from your house is 20 miles away. It will take you 5 minutes to walk from your car to the meeting room. What speed must you drive at to ensure you are on time?

    A. 70 mph

    B. 65 mph

    C. 80 mph

    D. 75 mph

    E. 60 mph

14. Farmer Sid collects bales of hay during his autumn harvest. In his first field he collects 43, in his second field he collects 62, in his third field he collects 13 and in his fourth field he collects 42. What is the average number of hay bales he collects from his fields?

    A. 39

    B. 40

    C. 41

    D. 42

    E. 37

15. There four new police recruits Mark, Laura, Ryan and Amy. Mark is 2 metres tall, Laura is 1.7 metres tall, Ryan is 1.8 metres tall, and Amy is 1.5 metres tall. What is the average height of the recruits in metres?

    A. 1.77 metres

    B. 1.68 metres

    C. 1.62 metres

    D. 1.70 metres

    E. 1.75 metres

16. Below is a bar chart showing daily book sales for four stores. How many books in total does Jay's Books sell.

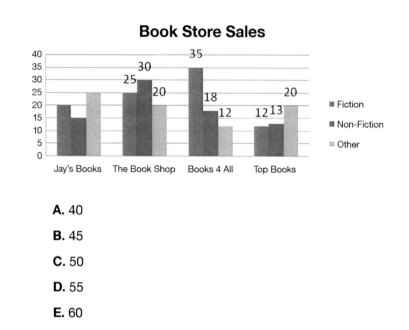

A. 40

B. 45

C. 50

D. 55

E. 60

17. What, on average, is the total amount of books sold at The Book Shop and Top Books?

A. 50

B. 55

C. 60

D. 75

E. 90

18. Whilst shopping you buy 6 items. You buy a steak costing £12.50, some vegetables costing £5.75, some cereal costing £1.21, some wine costing £10, some shampoo costing 42p and finally some sweets costing 12p. What is the average cost of the items you buy?

    A. £4

    B. £5

    C. £6

    D. £7

    E. £8

19. The distance between A and B is 140 miles. It takes you 4 hours to drive the distance. What speed have you been travelling at?

    A. 70 mph

    B. 40 mph

    C. 35 mph

    D. 30 mph

    E. 25 mph

20. You must arrive at work at 0900hrs. Your house is 6 miles from work. If you were to drive at 30 mph, what time would you need to leave the house to arrive at work on time?

    A. 0847hrs

    B. 0857hrs

    C. 0848hrs

    D. 0842hrs

    E. 0838hrs

21. On a Saturday night the police arrest 40 people. 22 are arrested for being drunk and disorderly, 10 are arrested for assault and 8 are arrested for drink driving. What percentage have been arrested for drink driving?

    A. 2%

    B. 5%

    C. 10%

    D. 20%

    E. 25%

22. During a daily patrol you average 12 miles at 3 mph. How long would it take to do a 14-mile patrol?

    A. 4 hours 50 minutes

    B. 4 hours 45 minutes

    C. 4 hours 20 minutes

    D. 4 hours 35 minutes

    E. 4 hours 40 minutes

23. A train is travelling from Birmingham to Glasgow covering a distance of 390 miles. If the train's speed is 90 mph, how long does the train journey last?

    A. 4 hours 20 minutes

    B. 4 hours 40 minutes

    C. 4 hours 10 minutes

    D. 4 hours 15 minutes

    E. 4 hours 30 minutes

24. You have 225 bags of sugar. If 15 bags of sugar fit in a box, how many boxes would you have in total?

    A. 10

    B. 12

    C. 13

    D. 15

    E. 20

25. Whilst hiking you walk a total distance of 725 miles over a 5-day period. On average, how many miles did you walk a day?

    A. 145 miles

    B. 150 miles

    C. 125 miles

    D. 90 miles

    E. 160 miles

PRACTICE TEST 10

1. An aircraft travels at a speed of 120 miles per hour over a total distance of 240 miles. How long does the journey take?

    A. 2 hours

    B. 4 hours

    C. 3 hours

    D. 2 hours 30 minutes

    E. 1 hour

2. How long does it take to drive 20 miles if you drive at a speed of 30 mph?

    A. 1 hour

    B. 20 minutes

    C. 40 minutes

    D. 45 minutes

    E. 50 minutes

3. A police officer walks for 15 miles in 3 hours. At what speed does the police officer walk?

    A. 45 mph

    B. 5 mph

    C. 20 mph

    D. 15 mph

    E. 10 mph

4. The distance between campsite A and campsite B is 32 miles. You walk at an average speed of 6 mph. If you set off from campsite A at 0900hrs, what time would you arrive at campsite B?

    A. 1520hrs

    B. 1410hrs

    C. 1440hrs

    D. 1610hrs

    E. 1420hrs

5. A train from Doncaster to Grimsby takes 1 hour 30 minutes. If the train is travelling at 64 mph, what is the distance travelled?

    A. 94 miles

    B. 96 miles

    C. 95 miles

    D. 92 miles

    E. 98miles

6. A yacht sails at 30 mph. You are sailing across the Channel estuary which is 240 miles long. How long does it take you complete your journey?

    A. 8 hours

    B. 5 hours

    C. 6 hours

    D. 4 hours

    E. 12 hours

7.   You find a rucksack full of money. In the bag there is a bundle of fifty £10 notes, a bundle of twenty £5 notes and ten money bags of £2 coins, each containing 15 coins. What is the total amount in the rucksack?

   A. 600

   B. 750

   C. 825

   D. 900

   E. 950

8.   You annual car insurance costs £240.48. How much is this per month?

   A. £20.04

   B. £20.02

   C. £18.04

   D. £22.02

   E. £22.06

9.   During a week of action, the Police carry out four early morning drug raids. On Monday they enter a property at 0710hrs and leave at 0720hrs. On Tuesday they enter at 0810hrs and leave at 0840hrs; on Thursday they enter at 0850hrs and leave at 0905hrs; and on Friday they enter a property at 0700hrs and leave at 0725hrs. What was the average time spent at a property during these raids?

   A. 10 minutes

   B. 25 minutes

   C. 20 minutes

   D. 30 minutes

   E. 45 minutes

10. The diagram below shows the floor plan of a house. Using the information supplied calculate the internal area of the house.

A. 880m²

B. 900m²

C. 1,155m²

D. 1,200m²

E. 1,245m²

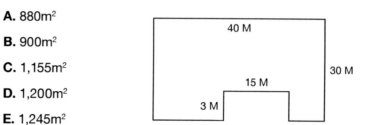

40 M

30 M

15 M

3 M

11. Using the plan above, calculate the perimeter of the house.

A. 145m

B. 146m

C. 148m

D. 152m

E. 156m

12. The train to work travels at 70 mph. The distance the train travels is 21 miles. How long does it take to travel to work?

A. 12 minutes

B. 8 minutes

C. 18 minutes

D. 15 minutes

E. 16 minutes

13. In your money box there are two £5 notes, five £2 coins, three £1 coins, six 10p coins and one penny. How much is in your money box?

    A. £23.61

    B. £13.61

    C. £14.61

    D. £16.41

    E. £23.41

14. A room is 12 metres long and 5 metres wide. A carpet tile is 100cm by 100cm. How many tiles do you need to carpet the entire room?

    A. 30

    B. 40

    C. 20

    D. 6

    E. 60

15. Bread costs £1.25, milk costs £2.13 and a pack of apples cost 66p. How much change will you have from £5?

    A. £0.94

    B. £0.96

    C. £1.06

    D. £1.36

    E. £1.96

16. A TV has been reduced by 20% to £200. What was its original price?

    A. £220

    B. £240

    C. £235

    D. £250

    E. £300

17. In Year 1 you had £200 in savings; by Year 2 this has increased to £230. By what percentage have your savings increased?

    A. 10%

    B. 12%

    C. 15%

    D. 20%

    E. 25%

18. House prices have decreased by 5%. The price of your house before the decrease was £150,000. What is its price now?

    A. £142,500

    B. £143,000

    C. £145,000

    D. £146,000

    E. £147,500

19. A car park has 8 floors. When completely full, each floor can hold 230 cars. How many cars in total can fit in the car park?

    A. 1,440

    B. 1,840

    C. 2,040

    D. 2,100

    E. 2,140

20. A police officer works 4 day shifts per week. How many days does a police officer (without holiday entitlement) work a year?

    A. 182

    B. 192

    C. 204

    D. 206

    E. 208

21. In one year, you arrest 321 people. 119 of these people are charged and the rest are cautioned. How many people are cautioned?

    A. 202

    B. 198

    C. 200

    D. 204

    E. 206

22. John is 6ft 2", Ben is 5ft 9", Sarah is 5ft 4" and Garry is 5ft 7". What is the average height of the group?

    A. 5ft 6"

    B. 5ft 7.5"

    C. 5ft 8.5"

    D. 5ft 9"

    E. 5ft

23. A farmer has 5 identical fields, all of which are square fields. If one side of a field measures 500 metres long, what is the combined total perimeter of all the farmer's fields?

    A. 1,000m

    B. 10,000m

    C. 25,000m

    D. 50,000m

    E. 100,000m

24. In a car park there are 1,200 cars. One sixth of the cars in the car park are blue. How many are blue?

    A. 20

    B. 100

    C. 200

    D. 250

    E. 400

25. In another car park there are 120 cars. Five tenths of the cars in the car park are red. Two thirds of the red cars have five doors. How many RED cars have five doors?

    A. 40

    B. 30

    C. 20

    D. 70

    E. 15

PRACTICE TEST ANSWERS

No	Test 1	Test 2	Test 3	Test 4	Test 5	Test 6	Test 7	Test 8	Test 9	Test 10
1	A	A	D	A	B	C	C	B	D	A
2	A	E	B	B	E	B	C	C	C	C
3	D	B	C	E	B	C	A	C	A	B
4	B	A	C	B	C	C	A	E	C	E
5	E	C	A	D	C	D	B	E	E	B
6	B	B	D	D	D	B	A	C	A	A
7	C	A	B	C	E	C	E	B	C	D
8	B	B	A	E	A	E	C	B	C	A
9	B	C	E	C	E	C	E	A	D	C
10	D	B	D	B	C	B	E	B	D	C
11	C	B	B	C	B	D	B	D	B	B
12	E	A	A	A	A	C	C	E	D	C
13	B	E	B	A	C	E	B	E	C	A
14	E	C	E	C	C	D	E	C	B	E
15	B	D	B	C	B	B	C	A	E	B
16	B	C	A	A	D	C	E	E	E	D
17	E	E	A	D	C	D	B	E	C	C
18	C	D	B	D	A	B	C	B	B	A
19	A	C	D	E	A	E	A	C	C	B
20	D	C	E	C	D	C	E	B	C	E
21	C	B	B	A	B	B	D	B	D	A
22	B	A	D	B	E	D	B	C	E	C
23	D	D	B	B	C	B	B	E	A	B
24	D	A	C	E	A	B	D	C	D	C
25	B	E	C	C	A	A	D	B	A	A

NUMERICAL REASONING PRACTICE TESTS
PART THREE

You will have 18 minutes to complete 10 questions.

You will be allowed to use a calculator during the numerical reasoning test.

QUESTION 1

Kent Police have put out a tender for electrical equipment and supplies.
Below are quotes from 3 suppliers.

Electrical Equipment and supplies	Supplier 1 Total cost over 2 years (£)	Supplier 2 Total cost over 2 years (£)	Supplier 3 Total cost over 1 years (£)
Basic Services	34,550	36,660	15,450
Electrical safety Check	39,550	42,000	20,000
Full Equipment Maintenance	120,850	150,500	60,000

1. Based on an annual year cost, which supplier offers the best price for electrical safety checks?

    A.   Supplier 1

    B.   Supplier 2

    C.   Supplier 3

    D.   They are the same

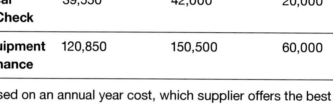
Answer

2. What percentage of the total quote provided by supplier 1 accounts for basic services?

    A.   17%

    B.   17.7%

    C.   18.5%

    D.   18.3%

    Answer

3. Based on 2 years, what supplier provides the cheapest quote overall for electrical equipment and supplies?

    A.   Supplier 1

    B.   Supplier 2

    C.   Supplier 3

    D.   Supplier 2 and 3

    Answer

QUESTION 2

Kent Police have put out a tender for heating maintenance and installation. Below are quotes from 3 supplier.

Heating maintenance and installation	Supplier 1 Total cost over 3 years (£)	Supplier 2 Total cost over 2 years (£)	Supplier 3 Total cost over 5 years (£)
Installation and boiler replacements	24,630	19,750	36,150
Hot Air Systems	142,530	102,640	229,850
Service and maintenance	17,880	12,460	25,625

1. Amongst all three suppliers, based on an annual cost, what is the average cost to install hot air systems?

   A.   45804

   B.   50000

   C.   48266

   D.   47655

   Answer [   ]

2. Based on 2 years, what supplier provides the most expensive quote for installation and boiler replacements?

   A.   Supplier 1

   B.   Supplier 2

   C.   Supplier 3

   D.   Suppler 1 and 3

   Answer [   ]

3. What percentage of the total quote provided by Supplier 2 accounts for hot air systems?

   A. 75%

   B. 76.1%

   C. 77.4%

   D. 73.9%

   Answer [   ]

QUESTION 3

The Police Headquarters have put out a tender for security checks and system updates. Below are quotes from 3 suppliers

Security checks and system updates	Supplier 1 Total cost over 2 years (£)	Supplier 2 Total cost over 4 years (£)	Supplier 3 Total cost over 5 years (£)
Basic Security Check	26,330	40,560	52,550
Advanced Security Check	52,530	104,320	120,880
Updating software and security	15,430	31,220	32,000

1. What percentage of the total quote provided by Supplier 2 accounts for updating software and security?

    A.   12.4%

    B.   17.7%

    C.   19.2

    D.   None of these

    Answer [   ]

2. For the total cost over 5 years, what supplier provides the cheapest quote overall for security checks and system updates?

    A.   Supplier 1

    B.   Supplier 2

    C.   Supplier 3

    D.   Supplier 1 and 2

    Answer [   ]

3. Based on an annual cost, what supplier provides the most expensive quote for basic security cost?

    A.   Supplier 1

    B.   Supplier 2

    C.   Supplier 3

    D.   All the same

    Answer [   ]

QUESTION 4

Kent Police have put out a tender for cleaning and support services. Below are quotes from 3 supplier.

Cleaning and support services	Supplier 1 Total cost over 2 years (£)	Supplier 2 Total cost over 3 years (£)	Supplier 3 Total cost over 4 years (£)
Basic cleaning services	15,050	19,850	22,500
Window cleaning	12,000	15,000	16,500
Specialist cleaning services	19,500	22,550	25,550

1. What is the average cost that suppliers charge for window cleaning?

    A.   14500

    B.   15000

    C.   16500

    D.   14000

    Answer [   ]

2. Based on a 2 year cost, which supplier is the cheapest for specialist cleaning services?

    A.   Supplier 1

    B.   Supplier 2

    C.   Supplier 3

    D.   All the same

    Answer [   ]

3. What percentage of the total quote provided by Supplier 3 accounts for basic cleaning services?

    A. 31.1

    B. 32.5

    C. 33.8

    D. 34.9

    Answer [   ]

QUESTION 5

The Police Headquarters have put out a tender for health and safety checks for staff. Below are quotes from 3 supplier.

Health and safety checks	Supplier 1 Total cost over 2 years (£)	Supplier 2 Total cost over 1 years (£)	Supplier 3 Total cost over 5 years (£)
Private Health check	36,880	18,000	53,500
Safety training	20,500	18,000	42,500
First aid training	22,500	12,000	42,000

1. Based on an annual cost, which supplier would be cheapest to provide first aid training?

    A.   Supplier 1

    B.   Supplier 2

    C.   Supplier 3

    D.   All the same

    Answer [   ]

2. Based on an annual one year cost, which supplier provides the most expensive overall quote for private health checks?

    A.   Supplier 1

    B.   Supplier 2

    C.   Supplier 3

    D.   All the same

    Answer [   ]

3. Based on an annual year, which supplier would provide the cheapest quote for an overall health and safety checks?

    A.   Supplier 1

    B.   Supplier 2

    C.   Supplier 3

    D.   All the same

    Answer [   ]

QUESTION 6

The Police Headquarters have put out a tender for fitness testing. Below are quotes from 3 supplier.

Fitness Testing	Supplier 1 Total cost over 2 years (£)	Supplier 2 Total cost over 3 years (£)	Supplier 3 Total cost over 4 years (£)
Basic Fitness Training	9,800	10,500	16,650
Intense Fitness Training	19,000	23,500	34,500
8 week Fitness Programme	16,000	18,000	33,000

1. What percentage of the total quote provided by Supplier 2 accounts for intense fitness training?

    A.   43.5

    B.   45.2

    C.   46

    D.   44.9

    Answer [   ]

2. Based on an annual one year cost, which supplier provides the most expensive overall quote for basic fitness training?

    A.   Supplier 1

    B.   Supplier 2

    C.   Supplier 3

    D.   Supplier 1 and 3

    Answer [   ]

3. Based on an annual one year cost, which supplier provides the cheapest 8 week Fitness programme?

    A.   Supplier 1

    B.   Supplier 2

    C.   Supplier 3

    D.   All the same

    Answer [   ]

QUESTION 7

Kent Police have put out a notice for staff to enrol onto the academic training course. Below are quotes from 3 suppliers.

Academic training course	Supplier 1 Total cost over 2 years (£)	Supplier 2 Total cost over 5 years (£)	Supplier 3 Total cost over 4 years (£)
English and vocabulary	12,500	28,000	25,500
Statistical Data	16,050	35,500	31,900
General knowledge	15,050	37,000	30,100

1. What percentage of the total quote provided by Supplier 2 accounts for statistical data?

   A.   30

   B.   35.3

   C.   36.1

   D.   35.2

   Answer [   ]

2. Based on an annual one year cost, which supplier provides the cheapest overall quote for English and vocabulary training?

   A.   Supplier 1

   B.   Supplier 2

   C.   Supplier 3

   D.   All the same

   Answer [   ]

3. Amongst all three suppliers, based on an annual cost, what is the average cost for statistical data training?

   A.   7500

   B.   7700

   C.   7900

   D.   8000

   Answer [   ]

QUESTION 8

Kent Police have put out a tender for computer software, security and updates. Below are quotes from 3 suppliers.

Computer software, security and updates	Supplier 1 Total cost over 2 years (£)	Supplier 2 Total cost over 3 years (£)	Supplier 3 Total cost over 4 years (£)
Computer downloads	12,550	22,000	41,480
System updates	16,350	19,500	32,750
Full system and computer check and updates	32,550	35,660	62,880

1. In an annual year, if supplier 1 were to have an order for 1 computer download, one system update, and a full system and computer check and updates, how much money would they earn?

    A.   £30500

    B.   £30900

    C.   £30700

    D.   £40000

    Answer

2. What percentage of the total quote provided by Supplier 3 accounts for full system and computer check and updates?

    A.   45%

    B.   45.9%

    C.   45.8%

    D.   45.6%

    Answer

3. Based on 2 years, which supplier provides the most expensive quote for system updates?

    A.   Supplier 1

    B.   Supplier 2

    C.   Supplier 3

    D.   All the same

    Answer

QUESTION 9

Kent Police have put out a tender for a charity event in order to raise money for their chosen charity every year. Below are quotes from 3 suppliers.

Charity event	Supplier 1 Total cost over 1 years (£)	Supplier 2 Total cost over 3 years (£)	Supplier 3 Total cost over 4 years (£)
Disco / Party	13,000	29,350	43,500
Fun fair	11,500	33,050	38,800
Outdoors assort course	12,000	35,800	40,500

1. Based on an annual one year cost, which supplier provides the cheapest overall quote for a disco/party charity event?

    A.   Supplier 1

    B.   Supplier 2

    C.   Supplier 3

    D.   All the same

    Answer [   ]

2. What percentage of the total quote provided by Supplier 3 accounts for outdoors assort course?

    A.   32.9%

    B.   33%

    C.   34%

    D.   33.3%

    Answer [   ]

3. Based on an annual year, what is the average cost that suppliers charge for hosting a fun fair?

    A.   10750

    B.   10738

    C.   10730

    D.   10739

    Answer [   ]

QUESTION 10

Kent Police have put out a tender for uniform dry cleaning and alterations. Below are quotes from 3 suppliers.

Uniform dry cleaning and amendments	Supplier 1 Total cost over 1 years (£)	Supplier 2 Total cost over 3 years (£)	Supplier 3 Total cost over 2 years (£)
Dry Cleaning	9,600	26,700	19,020
Alterations	5,500	14,900	11,000
Cleaning and alterations – Full package	13,450	38,850	25,800

1. Based on an annual one year cost, which supplier provides the cheapest dry cleaning services?

    A.   Supplier 1

    B.   Supplier 2

    C.   Supplier 3

    D.   All the same

    Answer [   ]

2. For the total cost over 3 years, what supplier provides the cheapest quote overall for cleaning and alterations – full package?

    A.   Supplier 1

    B.   Supplier 2

    C.   Supplier 3

    D.   All the same

    Answer [   ]

3. Based on an annual cost and everything the supplier has to offer, what supplier is the most expensive?

    A.   Supplier 1

    B.   Supplier 2

    C.   Supplier 3

    D.   All the same

    Answer [   ]

ANSWERS TO NUMERICAL REASONING QUESTIONS – SECTION 3

Question 1

1. Supplier 1

2. 17.7%

3. Supplier 3

Question 2

1. 48266

2. Supplier 2

3. 76.1

Question 3

1. 17.7%

2. Supplier 3

3. Supplier 1

Question 4

1. 14500

2. Supplier 3

3. 34.9

Question 5

1. Supplier 3

2. Supplier 1

3. Supplier 3

Question 6

1. 45.2

2. Supplier 1

3. Supplier 1

Question 7

1. 35.3

2. Supplier 2

3. 7700

Question 8

1. £30700

2. 45.9%

3. Supplier 3

Question 9

1. Supplier 3

2. 33%

3. 10738

Question 10

1. Supplier 2

2. Supplier 3

3. Supplier 1

REPORT WRITING EXERCISES

READ AND STUDY THE FOLLOWING SAMPLE REPORT WRITING
EXERCISE BEFORE FOLLOWING THE GUIDANCE ON HOW TO ANSWER
IT.

You are the customer services officer for a fictitious retail centre. Your
manager has asked you to compile a report based on a new pub that is
being opened in the centre. Your manager is meeting with the pub owners
in a few days' time to discuss a few issues and he wants you to write a
report based on the information provided. The pub owners have requested
that the pub is open to serve alcohol beverages in the centre from 11am
until 11pm.

At the bottom of this page there is a survey sheet that tells you that, on
the whole, the general public and staff are not happy with the idea of a
pub being opened in the shopping centre because of perceived antisocial
behavioural problems, littering and rowdiness.

It is your job to create a report for your manager stating what the main
issues are and what your recommendations would be.

SURVEY SHEET

The following information has been taken from a survey that was conducted
amongst 100 members of public who regularly shop at the centre and 30
employees who work at the centre.

- 60% of the general public and 80% of employees felt that the opening
  of a pub in the centre would increase littering.

- 80% of the general public and 60% of employees thought that
  rowdiness in the centre would increase as a result of the pub opening.

- 10% of the general public and 10% of employees thought that the opening of the pub would be a good idea.

On the following page there is an example of how the report could be written. There are many different recommendations that could have been made.

You should consider the information you have gathered and make the recommendation(s) you consider to be the best for those circumstances.

Remember: recommendations are suggestions for actions or changes.

They should be specific rather than general. It is important that you answer the question and state what your main findings and recommendations are.

SAMPLE RESPONSE TO WRITTEN EXERCISE

From: The Customer Services Officer
To: The Centre Manager
Subject: New pub

Sir,

Please find detailed my findings and recommendations in relation to the new pub as requested. The survey conducted took into the consideration the views and opinions of 100 members of the public and 30 members of staff who work at the centre.

Whilst a small proportion of staff and public (10%) felt that the opening of the pub would be a good idea, the majority of people surveyed felt that there would be problems with anti-social behaviour, littering and rowdiness.

Having taken into consideration all of the information provided, I wish to make the following recommendations:

The level of customer service that the centre currently provides is high and it is important that this is maintained. It is important to take into consideration the views and opinions of our customers and staff and to see things from their point of view. I believe that there would be a high risk involved if we were to allow the pub to serve alcoholic beverages from 11am until 11pm and that problems with anti-social behaviour could develop. We have a responsibility to protect the public and to ensure that they are safe whilst in the centre.

Whilst it is important to initially obtain the views of the pub owners, I recommend that the pub is only permitted to serve alcoholic beverages from 11am until 1pm and from 5pm until 7pm so as to reduce the risk of the above problems developing.

I have recommended this course of action, as I believe it is in the best interests of the centre, its staff and more importantly our valued customers. This alternative course of action would be for a trial period only and providing there are no problems with anti-social behaviour, littering or rowdiness we could look to review the opening hours with a view to extending them. I am prepared to take full responsibility for monitoring the situation once the pub has been opened. I will keep you updated on progress.

The Customer Services Officer

HOW TO CREATE AN EFFECTIVE REPORT
THE 5 STEP APPROACH

Now that you have read the sample response, take a look at the following 5 step approach that we use when creating a well structured report.

Step number 1 — Read the information provided in the exercise quickly and accurately

Remember that you only have 20 minutes in which to create your report. Therefore, you do not want to spend too long reading the information. We would suggest that you spend 2-3 minutes maximum reading the information.

Step 2 — Extract relevant information from irrelevant information (main findings)

When you read the information provided in the exercise you will notice that some of the information is of no significance. Write down which information is relevant in brief details only — these should be your main findings.

Step 3 — Decide what recommendations you are going to suggest or what action(s) you are going to take

One of the police officer core competencies is that of problem solving. If asked to, then you must come up with suitable recommendations. Do not 'sit on the fence', but rather provide a logical solution to the problem.

Step 4 — Construct your report in a logical and concise manner

You are being assessed on your ability to communicate effectively. Therefore you must construct your report in a logical and concise manner. You must also ensure that you answer the question.

Step 5 — Include keywords and phrases from the core competencies in your report

During each report or letter that you construct we strongly advise that you include keywords and phrases from the core competencies.

You will notice that the 5 step approach is easy to follow. Therefore I strongly suggest that you learn it and use it during the practise exercises that now follow. You have 20 minutes to complete each individual exercise.

WRITTEN REPORT EXERCISE 1

You are the customer services officer for a fictitious retail centre. Your manager has asked you to compile a report regarding a number of complaints he has received from shop owners who state that rowdy youths are intimidating shop owners at the centre which is having a detrimental effect on their business generally and more importantly their takings. Visitor numbers at the centre are down 25% over the last 3 months.

CCTV reports suggest that a gang of 8 youths have been circling the centre during daylight shopping hours, often approaching customers and harassing them for spare change.

The local newspaper have become aware of these incidents and they are sending a reporter along to interview your manager to see what the main problems are and what the centre intends to do about them.

Your report should detail your main findings and also your recommendations as to how the situation can be resolved.

Use the template on the following page to create your response.

WRITTEN REPORT EXERCISE 1 TEMPLATE

From —

To —

Title —

WRITTEN REPORT EXERCISE 2

You are the customer services officer for a fictitious retail centre. Your manager has received a request from the local council Anti Truancy Group who wish to patrol the centre in groups of 6 people for five day period next month.

During their request the Anti Truancy Group has raised concerns that school children from the local area are congregating at the retail centre during school hours. CCTV cameras have confirmed these reports.

Local police have also confirmed in a recent report that anti social behaviour in the area of the retail centre has increased by 15% in the last four weeks alone.

You are to create a report for your manager that details your main findings and your recommendations.

Use the template on the following page to create your response.

WRITTEN REPORT EXERCISE 2 TEMPLATE

From —

To —

Title —

WRITTEN REPORT EXERCISE 3

You are the customer services officer for a fictitious retail centre.

During a recent fire safety inspection at the retail centre, local Fire Officers found a large number of fire escapes blocked with cardboard boxes that had been stored by shop owners. They also noticed that many of the general areas were untidy and the housekeeping was below an acceptable standard. Whilst the obstructions were removed at the time of the inspection, and the Fire Service will not be taking any further action, your manager is concerned that this type of incident will happen again.

He has asked you to create a report detailing your recommendations as to how this type of incident can be prevented in the future and also how the standard of housekeeping can be improved.

Use the template on the following page to create your response.

WRITTEN REPORT EXERCISE 3 TEMPLATE

From —

To —

Title —

WRITTEN REPORT EXERCISE 4

As the customer services officer for a fictitious retail centre you are required to provide your Manager with a written report based on the following information.

Currently at the centre there are 3 unoccupied shops. A local charity would like to use one of the shops for a 3 month period free of charge in order to raise money for charity by selling second hand clothes and goods.

Your manager has already conducted a survey of all shop owners and staff at the centre to see what they feel about the proposal and the results are as follows:

- 15% of shop owners support the idea.
- 5% of shop owners do not have an opinion.
- 80% of shop owners are against the idea.
- 90% of staff at the centre support the idea.

You are to create a report detailing your main findings and recommendations based on the information provided.

Use the template on the following page to create your response.

WRITTEN REPORT EXERCISE 4 TEMPLATE

From —

To —

Title —

WRITTEN REPORT EXERCISE 5

You are the customer services officer for a fictitious retail centre.

Over the last 4 weeks the retail centre has been extremely busy and trade has been excellent. However, an issue has arisen whereby car owners are complaining that there are not enough car park spaces at the centre. Many of the shop owners are complaining that they are losing trade as many potential customers are turning their backs on the centre during busy periods due to the lack of car parking spaces.

A petition has been signed by every shop owner at the centre supporting the removal of the disabled car parking paces and reallocating them as standard car parking spaces in order to resolve the problem. There are currently 200 car parking spaces allocated at the centre specifically for disabled badge users.

Your manager is meeting with the shop owners in two days time to discuss their proposal. He wants you to create a report detailing the main issues and your recommendations.

Use the template on the following page to create your response.

WRITTEN REPORT EXERCISE 5 TEMPLATE

From —

To —

Title —

A FEW FINAL WORDS

You have now reached the end of the testing guide and no doubt you will be ready to take the Police Initial recruitment Test.

The majority of candidates who pass the police officer selection process have a number of common attributes. These are as follows:

1. They believe in themselves.

The first factor is self-belief. Regardless of what anyone tells you, you can become a police officer. Just like any job of this nature, you have to be prepared to work hard in order to be successful. Make sure you have the self-belief to pass the selection process and fill your mind with positive thoughts.

2. They prepare fully.

The second factor is preparation. Those people who achieve in life prepare fully for every eventuality and that is what you must do when you apply to become a police officer. Work very hard and especially concentrate on your weak areas.

3. They persevere.

Perseverance is a fantastic word. Everybody comes across obstacles or setbacks in their life, but it is what you do about those setbacks that is important. If you fail at something, then ask yourself 'why' you have failed. This will allow you to improve for next time and if you keep improving and trying, success will eventually follow. Apply this same method of thinking when you apply to become a police officer.

4. They are self-motivated.

How much do you want this job? Do you want it, or do you really want it?

When you apply to join the police you should want it more than anything in the world. You levels of self-motivation will shine through on your application and during your interview. For the weeks and months leading up to the police officer selection process, be motivated as best you can and always keep your fitness levels up as this will serve to increase your levels of motivation.

Work hard, stay focused and be what you want…

Richard McMunn

how2become

**Attend a 1 Day Police
Officer Training Course at**

www.PoliceCourse.co.uk